James Joyce

A Literary Life

Morris Beja

Ohio State University Press
Columbus

Published in the U.S.A. by Ohio State University Press.
Published simultaneously in Great Britain by The Macmillan Press Ltd.,
Houndsmills, Basingstoke, Hampshire RG21 2XS and London

Photos 1, 2, 10, 12, & 13 courtesy of Photography Collection, Harry Ransom Humanities Research Center, University of Texas at Austin;
11 & 15 courtesy of Carlton Lake Collection, Harry Ransom Humanities Research
Center, University of Texas at Austin (photo 15 by Gisèle Freund);
4, 5, 6, 7, 8, 9, & 14 courtesy of Cornell University Special Collections;
3 courtesy of Poetry/Rare Books Collection, University Libraries, State University of
New York at Buffalo.
Figure 16 courtesy of Ken Monaghan

Library of Congress Cataloging-in-Publication Data
Beja, Morris.
James Joyce : a literary life / Morris Beja.
p. cm.
Includes bibliographical references and index.

ISBN 0–8142–0599–2 (pbk. : alk. paper)
1. Joyce, James, 1882–1941—Biography. 2. Novelists, Irish—20th
century—Biography. I. Title.
PR6019.09Z525687   1992
823' .912—dc20
[B]   92–20068
                          CIP

Type set in Palatino
Printed by Braun–Brumfield, Inc., Ann Arbor, MI.

9   8   7   6   5   4   3   2

For Ellen

Contents

Preface: Imagination as Memory

O, you were excruciated, in honour bound to the cross of your own cruelfiction!

Finnegans Wake (192.17–19)

James Joyce's art was his 'cruelfiction' but also his salvation, and his triumph. Joyce led a triumphant and a sad life, constantly battling problems forced upon him and created by him.

He began his life within an affluent family and saw it decline into poverty and debt. As a youth he was popular – even a student leader – yet found himself feeling increasingly isolated within the world of his contemporaries. In a city he loved and knew intimately, he came to feel himself an 'exile'. He gave himself to his art with fanatic devotion, with the result that he was long unable to publish work which even those who presented obstacles to publication recognised as successful and important. He endured financial hardships until he began to receive – through earnings and patronage – enough funds to make him a wealthy man, although his spendthrift habits and the costs associated with his daughter's illness kept him constantly in financial difficulties. He worked long and hard on a book that was widely regarded as a masterpiece – and almost as widely thought of as obscene and dangerous, so that he once again faced censorship and could not publish the book in an English-speaking country for over a decade. He devoted even more years and more concentrated efforts to an even more ambitious work, to see many of his former admirers and supporters doubting its value, wondering if he was not wasting his genius.

He arrived nevertheless at a status in which he was recognised as a major force in world literature, only to have such recognition come at a time when, in his private life, he had to endure the agonies of a daughter with severe mental illness and a son without a career or sense of direction. Aside from his art, the most important thing in his life was his family, and he saw his children facing disintegration and unhappiness.

All these successes and all these problems contributed to the triumph of his art, for few artists have drawn so heavily – so clearly and in so much detail – on the fabric of their own lives in weaving their fictions. Fiction must not be confused with reality, autobiographical fiction with biographical 'truth'; yet the more we have come to learn about the smallest details of Joyce's life, the more we have come to see correspondences between that life and his art. 'The artist', his alter-ego Stephen asserts in *Stephen Hero*, 'affirms out of the fulness of his own life' (86). Or his attitude may be more negative: when Oliver St John Gogarty, the model for Buck Mulligan in *Ulysses*, requested in 1906 that they 'forget the past', Joyce's reply was that that was 'a feat beyond my power' (*LII* 183). In any case, Joyce was quite serious years later when he brushed aside some talk by his friend Frank Budgen about 'the question of imagination' with 'the assertion that imagination was memory' (*Myselves* 187). Again and again in this book we shall see how accurate that dictum was in his own case.

In *Ulysses*, as Stephen Dedalus explores the significance of Shakespeare's life for an understanding of his art, George Russell (AE) expresses his frustration at 'prying into the family life of a great man' – an approach, he claims, which is 'interesting only to the parish clerk'. Yet Joyce has planted this objection only after he has also made Russell remark, a few pages earlier, that 'the supreme question about a work of art is out of how deep a life does it spring' (155 [9.181–4], 153 [9.49–50]).

Throughout his literary career, Joyce was intensely devoted and committed to his craft, but he made relatively little money from his writing, and never enough for someone of his profligate habits to live on. During most of his professional life his chief sources of income came not from his books but elsewhere: from teaching, from patrons, or from a publisher whose financial arrangement with him was extraordinary. From the start his relationships with publishers were almost always unusual, perhaps even unique. Those relationships were sometimes contentious, as when one publisher would back away from a previous commitment to publish his work, or when another put out a garbled version of his work without his permission, in a pirated edition. But in key instances the role of the publisher was – even if Joyce somehow managed at times to make the relationship no less fiery – in contrast less like that of a publisher as such than that of a benevolent patron.

Joyce never doubted the appropriateness of such patronage. An essential aspect of his triumph was his confidence in his own art, and in his own genius – a confidence Stephen Dedalus does not always share, but with which he is permitted to end *A Portrait of the Artist as a Young Man*, as he goes out 'to forge in the smithy of my soul the uncreated conscience of my race' (253) – just as Joyce himself, in 1912, wrote to his wife that 'I am one of the writers of this generation who are perhaps creating at last a conscience in the soul of this wretched race' (*LII* 311). If such statements have a moral ring to them, that fact was not lost upon the hosts of writers whom he came to influence, sometimes profoundly. Samuel Beckett, for one, could recall in 1969, of his youth, that Joyce had had 'a moral effect' on him: 'he made me realize artistic integrity' (in Cohn 14).

While still at the University, Joyce had gone to a play with his parents, to whom he said, 'The subject of the play is genius breaking out in the home and against the home. You needn't have gone to see it. It's going to happen in your own house' (*MBK* 87). Such early confidence would seem to be hubris, except that it turned out to be justified (a fact which may not make it any more ingratiating). Even in those moments when he might acknowledge the possibility that he would not carry his work to full fruition, he never abandoned his sense of himself as an artist; as he wrote to his brother as early as 1905, 'it is possible that the delusion I have with regard to my power to write will be killed by adverse circumstances. But the delusion which will never leave me is that I am an artist by temperament' (*LII* 110). It was a conviction he never abandoned.

Morris Beja

Acknowledgements

It is impossible to become a biographer (the word in *Finnegans Wake* is 'biografiend') of James Joyce without some trepidation. In the general world of Joyce studies, no one can truly acknowledge all the scholarship and criticism from which one has learned and by which one has been influenced; the citations throughout this book will I hope in some measure indicate some of the greatest debts I owe to many scholars, critics, writers of memoirs, and biographers. In the specific realm of Joyce biography, nevertheless, one cannot help but recognise the special role played by Richard Ellmann: as editor of Joyce's letters and other volumes, but above all as biographer. The present volume cannot match the encompassing achievement of Ellmann's *James Joyce*, which remains the work to which a reader must turn for a detailed and comprehensive account of Joyce's life. This book must clearly have a more limited scope and focus, but it owes many debts to Ellmann's work even as it also attempts to reflect what has been learned – and thought – about James Joyce, his family, his writings and his world in the generation or more since Ellmann's biography first appeared. I am also grateful to Brenda Maddox, for both her life of Nora Joyce and her insights into the task of biography. For chances to think aloud about issues of biography, I would like to thank her and also Ira Nadel and Deirdre Bair.

Bernard Benstock originally suggested I take on this project, and I am grateful to him and to Shari Benstock as well for all our countless discussions of James Joyce over the years. The College of Humanities of the Ohio State University, and Dean G. Michael Riley, helped to support this project in several important ways.

A number of friends and colleagues read and commented upon all or parts of versions of this book in progress. I am indebted for suggestions to Mark Conroy, Frank Donoghue, Audrey Jaffe, Sebastian Knowles, Marlene Longenecker, Debra Moddelmog, Anne Neumann, James Phelan, Linda Raphael, Barbara Rigney and Arnold Shapiro. Especially extensive and helpful readings of entire drafts were provided by James Brown, Michael Gillespie, Richard Pearce and Charles Rossman – and by Ellen Carol Jones, to whom I dedicate this life.

Abbreviations

The following abbreviations have been used throughout this volume to indicate editions of Joyce's works and frequently cited secondary texts.

CW   Joyce, James. *The Critical Writings of James Joyce*. Ed. Ellsworth Mason and Richard Ellmann. New York: Viking, 1959.

DMW   Lidderdale, Jane, and Mary Nicholson. *Dear Miss Weaver: Harriet Shaw Weaver, 1876–1961*. New York: Viking, 1970.

D   Joyce, James. *Dubliners*. Ed. Robert Scholes in consultation with Richard Ellmann. New York: Viking, 1967.

E   Joyce, James. *Exiles*. New York: Viking, 1951.

FW   Joyce, James. *Finnegans Wake*. London: Faber and Faber, 1971.

JJ   Ellmann, Richard. *James Joyce*. Rev. ed. New York: Oxford University Press, 1982.

LI, LII, LIII   Joyce, James. *Letters of James Joyce*. Vol. I. Ed. Stuart Gilbert. New York: Viking, 1957; reissued with corrections, 1966. Vols. II and III. Ed. Richard Ellmann. New York: Viking, 1966.

MBK   Joyce, Stanislaus. *My Brother's Keeper: James Joyce's Early Years*. Ed. Richard Ellmann. New York: Viking, 1958.

N   Maddox, Brenda. *Nora: A Biography of Nora Joyce*. London: Hamish Hamilton, 1988.

P   Joyce, James. *A Portrait of the Artist as a Young Man*. Ed. Chester G. Anderson and Richard Ellmann. London: Penguin, 1980.

PAE   Potts, Willard, ed. *Portraits of the Artist in Exile: Recollections of James Joyce by Europeans*. Seattle: University of Washington Press, 1979.

SH   Joyce, James. *Stephen Hero*. Ed. John J. Slocum and Herbert Cahoon. New York: New Directions, 1963.

SL   *Selected Letters of James Joyce*. Ed. Richard Ellmann. New York: Viking, 1975.

U   Joyce, James. *Ulysses*. Ed. Hans Walter Gabler et al. New York: Random House, 1986; London: Bodley Head and Penguin, 1986.

1

As All of Dublin: The Years of Youth, 1882–1904

In him I have imaged myself. Our lives are still sacred in their intimate sympathies. I am with him at night when he reads the books of the philosophers or some tale of ancient times. I am with him when he wanders alone or with one whom he has never seen, that young girl who puts around him arms that have no malice in them, offering her simple, abundant love, hearing and answering his soul he knows not how.

Joyce, Epiphany #2[1]

The place where me heart was you could aisy rowl a turnip in,
It's as big as all of Dublin and from Dublin to the Divil's Glin.
. . .

'Pretty Molly Brannigan' (Irish ballad)

In James Joyce's life, as in his work, the concept of the family, and *his* family, were of primary importance. Throughout his adult life, like his own father before him, Joyce carried with him the family portraits, through all his wanderings and his many addresses. All the pictures, with the exception of one of his mother, were of the Joyces – that is, of James Joyce's paternal ancestors.[2]

Joyce was born 2 February 1882, at 41 Brighton Square West, in Rathgar, then a suburb of Dublin; the family was at that time fairly well-to-do, and a very good time it was. He was named James Augustine Joyce after his great-grandfather and grandfather (although in fact a mistake recorded the middle name as 'Augusta' in the birth records). His father, John Stanislaus Joyce, was born in 1849, in Cork.[3] Like many sons who have rebelled against their fathers, in later life James Joyce came more and more to identify with his.

Actually, Joyce's relationship with his father was less strained than Stephen Dedalus's with his – or than that of the rest of the children with John Joyce. The portrayal of Simon Dedalus in the

1

Portrait and *Ulysses* seems to some extent based on the perception of
John Joyce by James's siblings – in particular, his brother Stanislaus,
who regarded their father as 'lying and hypocritical', and as someone who had 'become a crazy drunkard' (*Diary* 6). In contrast, when
John Joyce died in 1931, James testified that 'I was very fond of him
always, being a sinner myself, and even liked his faults. Hundreds of
pages and scores of characters in my books come from him. His dry
(or rather wet) wit and his expression of face convulsed me often
with laughter' (*LI* 312). An example of that wit is recorded by Eugene
Sheehy, a friend of his son, who recalls that one day the elder Joyce
read the obituary of a Mrs Cassidy:

> Mrs. Joyce was very shocked and cried out:
> 'Oh! don't tell me that Mrs. Cassidy is dead.'
> 'Well, I don't quite know about that,' replied her husband, 'but
> someone has taken the liberty of burying her.'
>
> [In O'Connor 26]

Readers of *Ulysses* will recall that retort being worked on a bit and
attributed to Joe Hynes (247 [12.332–3]).

John Joyce had attended Queen's College in Cork, but unsuccessfully. With a small income from his father's will and from his maternal grandfather's bequest, he never acquired the ambition to work
very hard. When he moved to Dublin in his twenties, he tried various jobs of one kind or another (including one as advertising canvasser for the *Freeman's Journal*, a line of work his son was to provide
for Leopold Bloom in *Ulysses*). Perhaps with a degree of truth, he
blamed his loss of a position as tax collector at the Rates Office in
1891 on the political shifts arising from the fall of Charles Stewart
Parnell. In any case, he was compensated with a small pension: he
was in his early forties, and already responsible for supporting a
large family, yet for the rest of his life he never had another full-time
job. Stephen Dedalus describes his father in the *Portrait* as 'a medical
student, an oarsman, a tenor, an amateur actor, a shouting politician,
a small landlord, a small investor, a drinker, a good fellow, a story-
teller, somebody's secretary, something in a distillery, a taxgatherer,
a bankrupt and at present a praiser of his own past' (*P* 241); there
seems to be no exaggeration as one applies that description to John
Joyce.

John Joyce had married, in 1880, Mary Jane ('May') Murray, a
woman ten years younger than he. Her husband did not get along

with the Murrays, particularly with her brother William (*JJ* 19) – an ironic situation, since together the two men both contributed to the characterisation of the bullying, drunken father, Farrington, in Joyce's story 'Counterparts'. In his love for his mother, James was joined by the other children – although young Stanislaus could only record his feelings for his mother in his diary by contrasting them to those for his father; to Stanislaus, his mother was 'a selfish drunkard's unselfish wife' (*Diary* 10).

James was the oldest child. A daughter, Margaret ('Poppie'), was born in 1884, and a second son, John Stanislaus ('Stannie'), later that same year. The Joyces had ten surviving children, six girls and four boys; five others died in infancy. Of all his brothers and sisters, James was closest in most ways to Stannie, different as they were in personality (to James, called 'Sunny Jim' by the family, the serious and moral Stanislaus was 'Brother John'[4]). Stanislaus eventually served as a model for Mr Duffy in 'A Painful Case', for the brother Maurice in *Stephen Hero* and for Shaun in *Finnegans Wake* – but in his rebellion against their father and against Ireland, both much more severe in his life than in James's, he also contributed to the characterisation of Stephen Dedalus. In 1904 James wrote – more dramatically than truthfully – to his future wife, Nora, that 'my brothers and sisters are nothing to me. One brother alone is capable of understanding me' (*LII* 48). In that same year Stanislaus wrote that 'perhaps Jim owes something of his appearance to this mirror held constantly up to him. He has used me, I fancy, as a butcher uses his steel to sharpen his knife' (*Diary* 20). Also in 1904, within *Ulysses*, Stephen thinks of his brother – who otherwise is hardly a presence in either that novel or the *Portrait* – as his 'whetstone' (173 [9.977]).

James also had special affection for a younger brother, George, who was born in 1887 and died at the age of fourteen. The events leading up to that death, while James was a university student, produced one of the most moving of his 'epiphanies':

> [Dublin: in the house in
> Glengariff Parade: evening]
> Mrs Joyce – (*crimson, trembling, appears at the parlour door*) . . . Jim!
> Joyce – (*at the piano*) . . . Yes?
> Mrs Joyce – Do you know anything about the body? . . . What ought I do? . . . There's some matter coming away from the hole in Georgie's stomach. . . . Did you ever hear of that happening?
> Joyce – (*surprised*) . . . I don't know. . . .

Mrs Joyce – Ought I send for the doctor, do you think?
Joyce – I don't know. . . . . . What hole?
Mrs Joyce – (*impatient*) . . . The hole we all have . . . . . here (*points*)
Joyce – (*stands up*)[5]

A short while after George's death, Stanislaus heard James bitterly remark, 'Ireland is an old sow that devours her farrow' – an epigram Stephen will utter in both the *Portrait* and *Ulysses* (*P* 203; *U* 486 [15.4583]).

That view of his country was supported by what the Joyces and many others regarded as the 'betrayal' of Charles Stewart Parnell, whose efforts to achieve Irish freedom were doomed when many of his followers abandoned him after a divorce suit – at the height of his career and power, in 1889 – publicised his relationship with his married mistress, Kitty O'Shea. Prominent among those who turned against him was Tim Healy, formerly his close follower but then a major figure within the Church opposition to his leadership. The Catholic Church was a strongly conservative force upon Irish polit- ics, and it turned against the Protestant Parnell. Its attacks became so virulent that some priests refused to perform sacraments for Parnell's defenders, and one even threatened to turn a Parnell supporter into a goat! (Brown 343).

Parnell died 6 October 1891, shortly after his political downfall. For Joyce, Parnell's fate was all too typical; at the age of nine, he wrote a poem about it – since lost – significantly called 'Et Tu, Healy': the title's allusion to betrayal forecasts the adult Joyce's view of how 'this lovely land' in 'a spirit of Irish fun/ Betrayed her own leaders, one by one.'[6] Joyce ended an Italian essay he published in 1912, 'L'Ombra di Parnell' ('The Shade of Parnell'), by asserting that it redounds to the honour of Parnell's countrymen that when he appealed to them not to 'throw him as a sop to the English wolves . . . they did not fail his appeal. They did not throw him to the English wolves; they tore him to pieces themselves' (*CW* 228).

The divisions within Ireland were mirrored within the Joyce house- hold. John Joyce's uncle, William O'Connell, lived with the family in Bray, a seaside resort south of Dublin (where the Joyces lived from James's fifth to ninth years); so, for a time, did Mrs Hearn Conway, called 'Dante' by the children, whom she looked after and to some extent taught. Mrs Conway's husband had abandoned her, taking with him the fortune she had inherited from her brother. No doubt understandably bitter, she was also, Stanislaus claims, 'the most bigoted person I ever had the misadventure to encounter' (*MBK* 9). A frequent visitor to the home was John Kelly; he, like Mrs Conway, was a fervent patriot – but they disagreed furiously over the role of the Catholic Church in Parnell's fall, as reflected in the Christmas dinner scene in the *Portrait*, where Mr O'Connell appears as Uncle Charles, Mr Kelly as John Casey, and Mrs Conway as Dante. Unfortunately such arguments, not always political by any means, became more and more frequent within the household; according to Stanislaus's testimony, again, 'the house is and always has been intolerable with bickering, quarrelling and scurrility' (*Diary* 17).

James was his father's pride, and there was no question but that he would get the best – or the most prestigious – education available in Ireland. In later years, Joyce often expressed a gratitude and appreciation for his training that Stephen Dedalus, in contrast, seems reluctant to acknowledge. Perhaps above all Joyce was proud of the Jesuit character of his education; when Frank Budgen was writing his book on him, Joyce told him that while Budgen referred to him as a Catholic, 'to get the correct contour on me, you ought to allude to me as a Jesuit' (*JJ* 27).

He started that education exceptionally early. Clongowes Wood College, in County Kildare, among the oldest and then as now among the most distinguished schools in Ireland, normally took boys 'from the age of seven', according to its prospectus (*Workshop* 131); Joyce started there in 1888, at the age of six, and may still be the youngest child ever to have been admitted to Clongowes (Bradley 10). Nevertheless, he did well – even at sports, earning according to Stanislaus's testimony 'a sideboard full of cups and a "silver" (electroplate) teapot and coffee pot that he had won in the school hurdles and walking events' (*MBK* 41).

The rector at Clongowes was the 'mild, benign, rectorial' Father John Conmee (*U* 458 [15.3673]), who had been prefect of studies before taking on the job as rector as well; he was relieved of the former position in 1887 by Father James Daly, a man regarded as a martinet and feared by students throughout the thirty years he stayed at Clongowes. Daly arrived there from Limerick, where he had seen to it that 'the profession of idling was at an end among the boys'.[7] He has become infamous as the model for the Father Dolan in the *Portrait* who, accusing Stephen Dedalus of being a 'lazy idle little loafer' and not believing that the little boy had broken his glasses unintentionally, 'pandies' him (*P* 50). Like Stephen, Joyce appealed this unjust punishment to Father Conmee – and he too was upheld and assured that he would not receive any further punishment (Gorman 34). Because Father Daly administered the pandies in class, impromptu as it were, there is no record of them in the Clongowes *Punishment Book*, which survives and preserves an account of the more 'official' punishments; but the record does indicate that young James Joyce received several pandies during his years at Clongowes, including one prescient punishment for 'vulgar language' (Bradley 37).

His stay at Clongowes was cut short by the family's declining financial state in 1891. The Joyces were still at Bray that year, and the next they moved to another suburb, Blackrock, also to a nice home in a pleasant area. But the next year saw them move again, this time into the city proper, and then they had an astonishingly quick succession of moves, invariably to less desirable quarters, until by the time James was fifteen he had had a total of nine addresses; such an unsettled nomadic life would characterise his adulthood as well.

John Joyce had inherited a number of properties in Cork, but by 1894 – during the trip to Cork recorded in the *Portrait* – he had sold all of them. He had actually begun to sell them off more than a decade before that, but in his own mind – and to some extent in his son James's, in the family myth that has been called 'The Joycead' – 'the fall of John Joyce was part of the greater fall of Parnell' (Kearney 65). As one result of that fall, the family could no longer afford to send James to an expensive boarding school; in fact his plight was even harsher than Stephen Dedalus's, for he was sent to a Christian Brothers school on North Richmond Street, in the city – a prospect that Simon Dedalus vehemently rejects for *his* son: 'Christian brothers be damned! said Mr Dedalus. Is it with Paddy Stink and Mickey Mud? No, let him stick to the jesuits in God's name since he began with them' (*P* 71).

James's rescue came in 1893, when he was eleven, and once again his rescuer was Father Conmee, who had become prefect of studies at another eminent Jesuit school, Belvedere College, a non-boarding school within Dublin itself; he arranged for James and then his brothers to attend Belvedere as 'free boys'. That did not make them very unusual, since about a fourth of the students paid no fees (Bradley 86); nevertheless, in addition the rector, Father Henry, discreetly saw to it that James ate lunch at the rector's table, to make sure that he was well fed.[8]

Situated on a city street in northern Dublin, Belvedere provided a major contrast to Clongowes, which is in an old castle on its own large estate; but Belvedere too is a distinguished building architecturally; built in the eighteenth century, it is one of the finest Georgian structures in Dublin. Joyce was a good student, and he seems to have been especially fortunate in having been taught by an English teacher named George Dempsey, who may have been the most significant 'of all the intellectual influences on James Joyce in school' (Bradley 106). Certainly he recognised Joyce's abilities. William Fallon, a fellow pupil, reports that when the rest of the class was assigned to write on some lines from Pope's *Essay on Man*, Mr Dempsey told Joyce he could pick whatever topic he liked: the future author of *Ulysses* chose to write on Pope's translation of the *Odyssey* (O'Connor 42). Mr Dempsey formed the basis for Mr Tate in the *Portrait*, and the incident in that novel in which Mr Tate is 'appeased' after having accused his young student of 'heresy' seems actually to have occurred – as did the sequel, in which other students attempted to bully Joyce into naming an appropriate figure as 'the greatest poet', while he insisted on naming the rebellious Byron.[9]

Not all his experiences at Belvedere were so unpleasant: far from it. For example, at the age of sixteen he acted in a play, *Vice Versa*, in which he had the role of a headmaster – and he did not resist the temptation to burlesque the rector, Father Henry, in his portrayal. His impersonation caused the other actors to laugh so much they missed their cues – and produced a great deal of laughter from Father Henry too (Sheehy, in O'Connor 16–17).

In that era, there were important competitive examinations at the Intermediate (secondary) school level, with sizeable prizes of money. Newspapers treated the competitions 'like horse races or prize fights', and friends later remembered Joyce as having been 'one of the scholastic champions of his day' (Colum 13). That seems to be an exaggeration: he was rarely among the very top winners, but the amounts he won between 1894 and 1897 were nevertheless substantial for the time (for example, £20 in both 1894 and 1895, and £30 in 1897; John Joyce's annual pension totalled only £132); Joyce also received £3 in 1897 for the best composition by any student in his grade in all of Ireland (*JJ* 34, 40, 47, 51). That year, as the generally recognised 'head-boy' of Belvedere, he was elected prefect of the Sodality of the Blessed Virgin. But he became increasingly disaffected, and in his senior year, 1898, all his grades dropped to the lowest he ever attained (Bradley 132, 138).

By then, he had undergone a great many changes in his young life. At the age of fourteen, he was walking through a field with the family nanny when she asked him to turn around; he heard the sound of her urinating, and he was aroused – perhaps to masturbation. Apparently later that same year he had his first experience of sexual intercourse, with a prostitute he met while walking home from the theatre (*JJ* 418, 48). It was not his last experience with prostitutes. A large part of the fascination of those encounters for Joyce seems to have been the same as for Stephen, who 'wanted to sin with another of his kind, to force another being to sin with him and to exult with her in sin' (*P* 99).

For a time, this 'sinful' life co-existed with his sincere but agonised religious piety. Still when he was fourteen, in 1896, he was deeply affected by the annual retreat at Belvedere, conducted in late November and early December of that year by Father James Cullen, 'an almost morbidly introspective' priest who once confided in his diary that he dwelt too much 'on the swarming pestilential brood of my faults' (Bradley 124). Although Joyce used other models than Cullen's for the sermons in the *Portrait*, notably Pietro Pinamonti's *Hell Opened to Christians, To Caution Them from Entering It*,[10] he reacted much as Stephen Dedalus does to Father Arnall's. Two decades later Joyce was able to write a limerick making fun of the torments of damnation depicted by Father Cullen:

> *There once was a lounger named Stephen*
> *Whose youth was most odd and uneven.*
> > *He throve on the smell*
> > *Of a horrible hell*
> *That a Hottentot wouldn't believe in.*

[*LI* 102]

But the young Joyce did believe in it, and he was profoundly troubled by that belief. He attempted to reform his 'sinful' life, and he apparently succeeded for at least a few months (*JJ* 49).

His piety was noticed, and that – coupled with his achievements as a student – led to the suggestion, probably when he was sixteen, that he become a priest (Bradley 134–6). But by then there was little chance of his accepting the proposal, although lack of faith seems not to have been the cause of his refusal. Joyce later told friends that 'it was not a question of belief. It was the question of celibacy. I knew I could not live the life of a celibate' (Colum 134).

Whether because of his rejection of the priesthood, or out of some violent if belated reaction to the retreat, or for reasons we cannot now pin down, it seems to have been around that time that Joyce lost religious belief. In 1904, at the age of twenty-two, he wrote Nora Barnacle that 'six years ago I left the Catholic Church, hating it most fervently' (*LII* 48). He was not always to be so absolute in his description of his relation to the Church. In the 1920s Morris L. Ernst asked him 'when he had left the Catholic Church. He said, "That's for the Church to say." Which to me meant that inside himself he had never left the Church, try as he might have' (in Moscato 23). Ernst may have gone too far in his interpretation of Joyce's remark, but for the rest of his life Joyce remained profoundly influenced by the dogma, ritual, and processes of reasoning he had learned within the Church: the least that could be said of him is what Mulligan says of Stephen: 'you have the cursed jesuit strain in you, only it's injected the wrong way' (*U* 7 [1.209]).

Within *A Portrait of the Artist*, the connection between the question of celibacy and the vocation of the priesthood is symbolised by the vision of the wading girl on the beach of the Bull Wall, in northeastern Dublin – an incident that also occurred in Joyce's own life at that time (*JJ* 55). In the novel it also reveals to Stephen his true vocation, as it is prefaced by a realisation of the 'prophecy' in his 'strange name':

> . . . a prophecy of the end he had been born to serve and had been following through the mists of childhood and boyhood, a symbol of the artist forging anew in his workshop out of the sluggish matter of the earth a new soaring impalpable imperishable being.
> . . .

[P 169]

There is every reason to assume that Joyce, too, felt himself destined to be an artist around this time, although, as we have seen, he had begun to write poetry even by the age of nine. Stanislaus was to remember that James began a collaboration on a novel with a neighbour boy when they lived in Blackrock – that is, when James was ten or eleven. Stanislaus also recalls a series of 'sketches' (similar perhaps to the 'epiphanies' James would soon be writing) composed when his brother was sixteen or seventeen. The series was entitled *Silhouettes* after the first one, in which the narrator witnesses – through a window, with the light from within casting shadows on the lowered window blind – an argument between a bullying, apparently drunken husband and his wife, who a short time later warns her children, 'Don't waken Pa' (*MBK* 45, 90); the sketch suggests themes of family – particularly paternal – abuse he would eventually come back to treat masterfully in *Dubliners*, for example in 'Counterparts'.

At this time he was also a voracious reader, with an uncanny ability to remember huge passages of what he read. Decades later, while he was hospitalised for one of his many eye operations, he asked his friend Sylvia Beach to bring a copy of Scott's 'The Lady of the Lake' on her next visit. When she did so, he asked her to pick any line at random and read it aloud:

> After the first line, I stopped, and he recited the whole page and the next without a single mistake. I'm convinced that he knew by heart, not only 'The Lady of the Lake', but a whole library of poetry and prose. He probably read everything before he was twenty, and thenceforth he could find what he needed without taking the trouble of opening a book.
>
> [Beach 71]

In his late adolescence, Joyce's chief intellectual passion was for Henrik Ibsen, the Norwegian dramatist who was by then in his early seventies and, although famous on the continent and in England, not yet widely known in Ireland. Joyce retained his enthusiasm into his university days, when he published an essay on 'Ibsen's New Drama', *When We Dead Awaken*, in the extremely prestigious *Fortnightly Review* at the age of eighteen. Joyce's university friend J. F. Byrne has testified that 'it would be impossible for a young collegiate of the present day to realise the importance attached in Joyce's time by some persons, in certain circles, to the *Fortnightly Review*' (61). Joyce was even more elated when a letter came from William Archer, Ibsen's English translator, conveying Ibsen's thanks for the article; in his reply to Archer, Joyce wrote, 'I am a young Irishman, eighteen years old, and the words of Ibsen I shall keep in my heart all my life' (*LII* 7). The next year, 1901, Joyce wrote to Ibsen himself on his seventy-third birthday; the letter reveals a conscious and passionate identification with the older genius:

> I have sounded your name defiantly through a college where it was either unknown or known faintly and darkly. I have claimed for you your rightful place in the history of the drama. I have

shown what, as it seemed to me, was your highest excellence –
your lofty impersonal power. . . .

. . . Your work on earth draws to a close and you are near the
silence. . . .

As one of the young generation for whom you have spoken I
give you greeting – not humbly, because I am obscure and you in
the glare, not sadly because you are an old man and I a young
man, not presumptuously, nor sentimentally – but joyfully, with
hope and with love, I give you greeting.

[*LI* 51–2]

Joyce always remained loyal to his admiration for Ibsen, and in later
years argued that 'Ibsen has been the greatest influence on the present
generation. . . . His ideas have become part of our lives even though
we may not be aware of it' (Power 35).

One of Joyce's epiphanies centres on a parlour game in which his
friends wanted him to guess Ibsen's name, but got some facts wrong,
in an incident Joyce thought significant enough to use in *Stephen
Hero* as well:

[Dublin: at Sheehy's, Belvedere
Place]
Joyce – I knew you meant him. But you're wrong about his age.
Maggie Sheehy – (*leans forward to speak seriously*) Why, how old is
he?
Joyce – Seventy-two.
Maggie Sheehy – Is he?[11]

The epiphany is one of several that record fragments of the parlour
games played at the home of the Sheehys (the Daniels of *Stephen
Hero*), the fairly prominent family of a member of Parliament at
Westminster. Joyce was welcome at their home, and became especially friendly with one of the sons, Richard, and also with Eugene,
who has written a short memoir about their friendship. Joyce had a
bit of a crush on Mary, one of the four daughters in the family.
Another daughter, Margaret, wrote a play which was put on in 1900;
Joyce played the role of the villain (*JJ* 93).

In 1898, at the age of sixteen, Joyce matriculated at University
College, Dublin: he was the only one of all the Joyce children to
attend university. University College, founded by John Henry
Newman in 1853, had begun as the Catholic University and was still

run by Jesuits; it was not as prominent an institution of higher learning, at the time, as Trinity College, the Protestant university, also in the centre of the city. Among its faculty were Thomas Arnold, the Professor of English and the brother of Matthew Arnold, and Father Charles Ghezzi, who taught Italian and appears in Joyce's work both under his own name and as Almidano Artifoni. Joyce was fond of Ghezzi, and learned a great deal from him about Italian literature, in which he became intensely interested. But it was with Ghezzi that he had the conversation about Giordano Bruno in which the priest observed that it must not be forgotten 'that he was a terrible heretic' – to which Joyce, like Stephen Dedalus, replied that he would also remember 'that he was terribly burnt'.[12]

Bruno, the sixteenth-century philosopher from Nola, was 'the Nolan' in the opening sentence of an essay Joyce wrote in 1901, in a reference which perplexed his readers and which was often repeated and made fun of by his friends: 'No man, said the Nolan, can be a lover of the true or the good unless he abhors the multitude; and the artist, though he may employ the crowd, is very careful to isolate himself' (*CW* 69). In what was already not his first bout with censorship, Joyce could not get his unpopular views published in *St Stephen's*, a new university magazine. Two years earlier a fellow student had attempted to prevent him from reading another paper, 'Drama and Life', before the Literary and Historical Society (*JJ* 70–1). This time he combined forces with Francis Skeffington, who had also had trouble publishing an essay – a feminist argument for equal rights for women – and they published the two articles together in a small pamphlet in 1901.

Joyce's essay, combatively entitled 'The Day of the Rabblement', was inspired by his reaction against what he regarded as the feeble insularity of the Irish Literary Theatre (later the Abbey Theatre). In contrast, two years beforehand William Butler Yeats's play *The Countess Cathleen* had caused protests and great controversy; Joyce boasted (unjustly) that he was 'the only student' who 'refused to sign the letter of protest against *Countess Cathleen* when I was an undergraduate' (*LI* 98). By the time he wrote 'The Day of the Rabblement' Joyce lamented that Irish theatre had become unworthy to follow in the tradition of Ibsen – although 'his successor', the budding artist self-reflexively asserts, 'will not be wanting when his hour comes. Even now that hour may be standing at the door' (*CW* 70, 72).

The later Joyce encouraged the sense of his aloofness and aloneness at this time; the first biography of Joyce, written more or less under his supervision by Herbert Gorman, asserts in regard to his university days that 'Joyce did not need friends; he was quite sufficient unto himself; and the minds to whom his own kindled were not plentiful in Dublin' (59). There is no doubt a measure of accuracy in this portrayal, for Joyce always went his own way. Even his course of study was unusual for a male student; Mary Colum remembers hearing that Joyce's degree was 'in modern languages as if he were a girl student, for the girls at this time were supposed to be specialists in modern languages and literature, while the boys' domain was classics, mathematics, and similar masculine pursuits' (12). Certainly, too, Joyce was noticed and stood out; another of his essays, delivered before the university's Literary and Historical Society, was described in the report in the *Freeman's Journal* as one that 'was generally agreed to have been the best paper ever read before the society' (*Workshop* 153).

Nevertheless, the picture of Joyce as without friends is misleading – as is the sense that there were no kindred spirits among the students at the university. One of his friends, Constantine P. Curran, has written that he finds himself 'bewildered' as he searches his memory 'in vain for those pathetic figures, devoid of intellectual curiosity, not merely docile but servile' (58), whom he perceives – in what in itself is not a totally accurate reflection of the novel – as he reads the *Portrait*; other memoirs too support Curran's picture of an intellectually active and exciting group of peers.

Francis Skeffington, with whom Joyce shared his pamphlet, was acknowledged by Joyce to be 'the most intelligent man' at the university – 'after myself' (*MBK* 145). The model for MacCann in the *Portrait*, Skeffington led a full and interesting life brutally cut short during the Easter Rebellion in 1916, when he was summarily executed by a British officer later judged as insane. By then, faithful to his feminist principles, he had changed his name to Francis Sheehy-Skeffington, when he married Hannah, one of the Sheehy sisters.

Joyce's closest friend during his university days was J. F. Byrne (the model for Cranly in the *Portrait*); he too has published a memoir of his times with Joyce, who, hearing in 1940 that Byrne had written a book, remarked to Mary Colum that 'I should have been surprised to hear that he had read one' (*LI* 411). Byrne, as unusual in his own way as Joyce, may not have seemed to his friend to be especially intellectual in his interests, but he was an intelligent young man – and a perceptive and willing listener. He could also be touchy; for reasons he would not disclose in his autobiography, he once broke with Joyce, apparently over both Joyce's behaviour with prostitutes in Paris and his willingness to report those experiences in a slightly bawdy postcard to Vincent Cosgrave, another friend of Joyce's and one whom Byrne did not trust (*JJ* 116). For his part, at this point Joyce needed the continued friendship and refused to be broken with (Byrne 84–5). A few years later, in 1904, however, Joyce wrote to Nora Barnacle, apparently in reference to Byrne, that 'when I was younger I had a friend to whom I gave myself freely – in a way more than I give to you and in a way less. He was Irish, that is to say, he was false to me' (*LII* 50). Yet, as we shall see, Byrne was to perform a great service to Joyce five years after that: one which helped to save his relationship with Nora, when it was threatened by lies Cosgrave had told.

At home, the family situation was now worse than ever, as the Joyces moved with greater frequency, to ever more depressing homes and neighbourhoods; their financial plight was magnified as Mr Joyce mortgaged much of his pension to pay for housing; James himself was faced with the need to earn money, despite his belief, reported in Stanislaus's diary, that 'he should be supported at the expense of the State because he is capable of enjoying life' (26). Until that could be arranged, Joyce had to contemplate some type of profession. Despite his lack of talents in that direction, he chose medicine, perhaps because the long tradition of poet-doctors enabled him to believe that his true ambition, to be an artist, would not have to be abandoned while he merely made a living. Oliver St John Gogarty has summarised Joyce's plight at that time: 'His father was an alcoholic, an old alcoholic wag. His mother was a naked nerve; and Joyce himself was torn between a miserable background and a sumptuous education' (*It Isn't This Time* 90). Gogarty must have provided a prospective example of what Joyce envisioned; at the time a medical student, he did in fact go on to combine prominent literary and medical careers.

So Joyce began his medical training in October 1902, after having attained his BA in Modern Languages in June. Within a month, the plan was not working out; he had special trouble with chemistry (as he testified later, 'I never could learn it or understand what it is about' [*SL* 249]). Typically, Joyce used his problems at medical school to persuade himself to do what he really wanted to do, so he decided against all odds and logic to go to Paris and set up as a medical student there, apparently ignoring the possibility that having to learn technical subjects in a foreign language might compound his difficulties. (For most other purposes, his French was fluent; he also knew very well Italian, German, and Latin, and a bit of Irish; and he had studied Norwegian in order to read Ibsen in the original language.) In response to a quick query to France in regard to admission, he was told by the Faculté de Médecine that nothing could be decided yet (*JJ* 106) – information which for some reason he interpreted as evidence that he should go to Paris immediately. Having borrowed and scraped up enough money for the journey, with hardly anything to spare, he left 1 December 1902.

On the way, he stopped in London, where he was kindly greeted by William Butler Yeats, although Joyce did not really know the older poet very well; Lady Gregory had written to Yeats asking him to see what he could do for the impetuous young man who had gone to her for help in his plans to leave Ireland. Yeats brought him to the offices of journals that might offer him the opportunity to review books, and arranged a meeting with Arthur Symons, a poet, editor and influential critic who had helped introduce the French Symbolists to the English in his 1899 volume, *The Symbolist Movement in Literature*. Symons would eventually help Joyce publish his poetry.

Joyce completed his trip to Paris by boat and train. He seems to have attended some classes within a week, but by 21 December he wrote to Lady Gregory that 'my prospects for studying medicine here are not inviting' (*SL* 11). The problem was poverty as well as chemistry. He attempted to earn some money giving English lessons, but he went through prolonged periods of fasting, which made him ill (*LII* 31). His worried mother – who had warned him 'against drinking the water of Paris unless it is either well-filtered or boiled. Don't forget this' (*LII* 20) – was the recipient of letters that could only serve to increase her anxiety:

> My next meal . . . will be at 11 a.m. tomorrow (Monday): my last meal was 7 pm last (Saturday) night. So I have another fast of 40 hours – No, not a fast, for I have eaten a pennyworth of dry bread. My second last meal was 20 hours before my last. 20 and 40 = 60 – Two meals in 60 hours is not bad, I think.
>
> [*LII* 34]

It was no wonder that he had already decided to try to return home for the Christmas holidays within weeks of having arrived in Paris – or that his parents had mortgaged their home to send him the money for the trip back to Dublin (*JJ* 114). But he returned to Paris in January 1903, and he stayed until April, when his mother, who had been ill, turned worse. He sent her a frightened postcard asking her to 'please write to me at once if you can and tell me what is wrong' (*LII* 41). The next day he borrowed money from a pupil (Joseph Douce, whose name deserves to be recorded) and rushed home; he had received a telegram like the one Stephen remembers receiving in *Ulysses*: 'Mother dying come home father.'[13]

Italo Svevo, the brilliant Italian novelist who knew him in Trieste, came to believe that Joyce's frequent pugnaciousness could be explained because he was 'essentially a mother's boy, who did not expect to find hostility in the world and was extravagantly indignant when he encountered it' (Furbank 84). Joyce's sister testified, in regard to his relationship with his mother, that 'Jim was completely dependent on her not only for a mother's care, but especially for moral support. He wanted her to believe that he would make a success of his life as a writer.'[14] That view is supported by their letters. From Paris he had written her of his plans for his art: 'My book of songs will be published in the spring of 1907. My first comedy about five years later. My "Esthetic" about five years later again. (This *must* interest you!)' (*LII* 38). Her reactions to such appeals were sincere and moving:

> My dear Jim if you are disappointed in my letter and if as usual I fail to understand what you would wish to explain, believe me it is not from any want of a longing desire to do so and speak the words you want but as you so often said I am stupid and cannot grasp the great thoughts which are yours much as I desire to do so.
>
> [*LII* 22]

Mrs Joyce had been the force holding the family together, and she now had cancer. Her illness was prolonged, and her husband, unable to handle the consequent pressures, one day shouted to her from the foot of her bed, 'I'm finished. I can't do any more. If you can't get well, die. Die and be damned to you!' Stanislaus, furious, lunged towards him but stopped when he saw his mother struggling to get out of bed to prevent him from confronting his father; James led the older Joyce out of the room.[15]

The two brothers, however, also had trouble being as generous-hearted to their dying mother as they would have wished. James had to refuse her request that he take communion (*JJ* 129), and Stanislaus's rejection of Catholicism had become even more violent than his older brother's. When Mrs Joyce's brother John knelt at her deathbed

in her last moments, while she was unconscious and therefore unaware, he saw that her sons were not praying and gestured for them
to kneel down. 'Neither of us paid any attention to him', Stanislaus
reports, 'yet even so the scene seems to have burnt itself into my
brother's soul' (*MBK* 234). Joyce made Stephen Dedalus's decision
more extreme, for it is Stephen's mother, not an uncle, who makes
the same request, and of him alone: 'You could have knelt down,
damn it, Kinch, when your dying mother asked you, Buck Mulligan
said. . . . To think of your mother begging you with her last breath to
kneel down and pray for her. And you refused. There is something
sinister in you . . .' (*U* 5).

Joyce felt additional sources of his own guilt towards his mother.
He believed that she was 'slowly killed . . . by my father's ill-
treatment, by years of trouble, and by my cynical frankness of conduct', and when he looked on her face in her coffin 'I understood
that I was looking on the face of a victim and I cursed the system
which had made her a victim' (*LII* 48). Her death came 13 August
1903, after a long illness but while she was still fairly young: although she had undergone fifteen pregnancies, she was only forty-
four. Joyce, who had been unable to pray for her himself, calmed his
nine-year-old sister Mabel's grief by assuring her that their mother
was in heaven, and that Mabel could pray for her: 'Mother would
like that' (*MBK* 237).

The effect of her death on the family was devastating. Much of
the responsibility for attempting to hold things together fell on the
oldest daughter, Margaret ('Poppie'), but Mr Joyce was of little help,
and the family members began to scatter. Many of them, however,
found a needed welcome in the home of their mother's sister-in-law,
Josephine Murray, the wife of William Murray, Mrs Joyce's brother.
Aunt Josephine was herself the mother of four daughters and two
sons, but her home was always open to the Joyce children, and they
were grateful and took advantage of her sympathy and warmth.
Stanislaus even showed her part of his diary, remarking in it later,
'Charlie used to tell her all his boring mind and his worse verse, Jim
tells her practically everything, and here am I now' (66). In fact no
one turned to her more intensely than James, who transferred to her
much of the role his mother had played in his life, including many of
the demands for comfort and approval. Those demands persisted for
decades; when he had published *Ulysses* and sent her a copy, he was
disturbed at her confession that she found it difficult and had not
read it; he arranged to have a critical article on it sent to her and

advised her to read Lamb's *Adventures of Ulysses*: 'Then have a try at *Ulysses* again', he pleaded (*LI* 193).

For a very short time in 1904 he even lived with William and Josephine Murray, but that in itself does not mean a great deal, since he changed his address repeatedly once he returned from Paris and rarely lived in his father's home. He was notably lonely – the full intimacy with Byrne was over, although they remained friendly enough – and only fitfully employed. One of his jobs, lasting only several weeks, was as an assistant teacher at the Clifton School, in Dalkey, south of Dublin and near Sandycove. The headmaster of the private school, Francis Irwin, helped contribute to the characterisation of Mr Deasy in *Ulysses* (*JJ* 153).

Although, as it turned out, for much of his life Joyce made his living as a teacher, during this period he took more seriously the possibility of a singing career. He had a fine tenor voice, of which he always remained proud; in 1903 friends encouraged him to enter a singing contest, and after some voice lessons he sang in the competition – in a *Feis Ceoil* – in May; he would have won the gold medal except for the fact that when he was given a short piece to sight-read, an ability beyond Joyce's musical education, he declined and walked off the stage; in the end he won the bronze medal anyway, and he gave it to Aunt Josephine (*JJ* 152). He was sufficiently encouraged by the reception he had received to think of making the same sort of concert tour of the English coast that Bloom will daydream about for Molly: 'I am trying to get an engagement in the Kingstown Pavilion. . . . My idea for July and August [1904] is this – to get Dolmetsch to make me a lute and to coast the south of England from Falmouth to Margate singing old English songs.'[16] The plan was impractical if only because of costs (Joyce could not even afford the lute). Nevertheless, he continued to sing; one Dubliner, Joseph Holloway, recorded in his diary for 8 June 1904 hearing him at a private home:

> Then Mr J. Joyce, a strangely aloof, silent youth, with weird, penetrating eyes, which he frequently shaded with his hand and with a half-bashful, far-away expression on his face, sang some dainty old world ballads most artistically and pleasingly. . . . Later he sat in a corner and gazed at us all in turn in an uncomfortable way from under his brows and said little or nothing all the evening. He is a strange boy. I cannot forget him. . . .
>
> [*Workshop* 163–4]

In August, Joyce shared a platform with John McCormack at the

Antient Concert Rooms (where Molly Bloom is also said to have sung); one of the songs Joyce sang was 'The Croppy Boy'. Holloway was there too, and he records a problem with the accompanist that looks forward to the *Dubliners* story 'A Mother'.[17]

One day around this time Joyce met, in the National Library, Oliver St John Gogarty, four years older and from a prosperous Dublin family. In contrast to the impoverished, drifting Joyce, Gogarty was clearly destined for a successful career: already gaining a reputation for his cleverness and wit, he had been to Oxford, was a poet, and went on to a career as a well-known surgeon – although in an irony always thereafter bitter to him he gained his chief fame as the source for Buck Mulligan in *Ulysses*. His influence on Joyce was not always beneficent; for example Joyce, until he met Gogarty, did not drink very heavily – but that began to change, and apparently the shift was part of an effort by Gogarty, in his own words, to 'make Joyce drink to break his spirit' (*JJ* 131).

Part of Gogarty's influence clearly came from the interests and traits they shared, but in essential ways they were also very different. For one thing, Gogarty was a snob, while Joyce, according to Gogarty, 'had the formal and diffident manners of a lay brother in one of the lower orders of the Church' (*It Isn't This Time* 91). One manifestation of Gogarty's snobbery was anti-semitism; in 1906 he published in *Sinn Féin* an attack on the 'Jew mastery of England' in which he claimed he could 'smell a Jew . . . and in Ireland there's something rotten'.[18] For Joyce, when he read it, the piece was an example of 'O.G.'s stupid drivel' (*LII* 200). More than thirty years later, incidentally, a Jewish citizen of Dublin, Henry Morris Sinclair, sued Gogarty for libel and was awarded £900; among the witnesses for Sinclair and against Gogarty was Samuel Beckett. By then *Ulysses* had appeared, of course, and in it Bloom refers to 'young Sinclair' as a 'wellmannered fellow'.[19]

On 9 September 1904, Joyce began living with Gogarty in about as strange a home as one could come up with in all of Ireland: the Martello Tower, in Sandycove. Scores of such military towers had been built along the coast by the British early in the nineteenth century, amidst concern over a possible invasion by French forces to liberate Ireland from the English. Now, realising their obsolescence as defence garrisons, the War Office had begun renting them out. The one where Gogarty and Joyce lived is today the James Joyce Museum and has been renovated for that purpose; Gogarty provides a description of what it was like when Joyce and he were there:

The Tower at Sandycove is built of clear granite. It is very clean. Its door, which is halfway up, is approached by a ladder fixed beneath the door, which is opened by a large copper key, for there was a powder magazine in the place and the copper was meant to guard against sparks which an iron key might strike out from the stone. There is a winding staircase in the thickness of the wall to the side that does not face the sea. On the roof, which is granite, is a gun emplacement, also of granite, which can be used for a table if you use the circular sentry walk for a seat.

[*It Isn't This Time* 86]

In *Ulysses* it is not clear who pays the rent for the tower; for some reason Gogarty always said it was Joyce who paid theirs, but the evidence indicates that Gogarty paid it, with the understanding that – as Gogarty wrote in a letter before they moved in – Joyce would do the housework as he took 'a year in which to finish his novel'.[20] The arrangement does seem to have been Joyce's 'great idea' (Gogarty, *Mourning* 43). There was a third person in the tower, as a visitor: Samuel Chenevix Trench (the model for Haines in *Ulysses*), whom Gogarty had known at Oxford. Trench, who had an independent income, was an enthusiast for the Irish language. He eventually committed suicide, perhaps with the same revolver with which Gogarty precipitated the crisis in his friendship with Joyce (*JJ* 175).

That relationship had already been strained; a couple of weeks before they were together in the tower, Gogarty wrote a friend that he had 'broken with Joyce' (*Many Lines* 33). On 14 September Stanislaus conjectured in his diary that 'Gogarty wants to put Jim out' of the tower, 'but he is afraid that if Jim made a name someday it would be remembered against him (Gogarty) that though he pretended to be a bohemian friend of Jim's, he put him out. . . . Jim is determined that if Gogarty puts him out it will be done publicly' (85–6). That very night, Trench had a nightmare and shouted 'the black panther!' – and then shot his revolver toward the grate. Joyce was, naturally, extremely frightened; Trench fell back asleep, and Gogarty removed the gun. When Trench again shouted about the black panther, Gogarty took up the revolver himself and 'shot down all the tin cans on the top of Joyce' (*Mourning* 56–7). In silence, the furious Joyce left the tower in the middle of the night; he had been there only five days.[21]

This experience helped produce in Joyce a personal sense of betrayal comparable to the one he had long perceived in Irish politics. As he announced with self-perception to Stanislaus the next year, he seized upon a 'youthfully exaggerated feeling' of 'falsehood' on the part of friends and relatives as 'an excuse for escape' (*LII* 89). Apparently he decided to make his escape upon leaving the tower, for it seems to have been the following night that he proposed to Nora Barnacle that they elope (*N* 62).

Faced with all the falsehood and treachery he sensed in the male world around him, Joyce began to believe that loyalty might be found in women; in a 1906 letter to Stanislaus he credited two women – Aunt Josephine and Nora – with an ability 'to understand me' and 'a certain loyalty which is very commendable and pleasing' that he could not find in his male friends (*LII* 157). He came indeed to feel that, as he mentioned many years later to one woman friend, Carola Giedion-Welcker, 'again and again in life it has been women who were most active in helping me' (*PAE* 256). He was of course right: there were his mother, his Aunt Josephine, and as we shall see there were also, notably, Sylvia Beach and Harriet Shaw Weaver, as well as other women important in publishing his works, like Margaret Anderson, Jane Heap, and Adrienne Monnier (as Beach once remarked, 'it was always women who were publishing Joyce'[22]), and friends such as Maria Jolas. So while Joyce all too often took on the pose of a man who hated 'women who know anything', as he once claimed to Mary Colum, she was surely correct in replying immediately, 'No, Joyce, you don't. . . . You like them.'[23]

Although actively intellectual and artistic women do not play a major role in his fiction, in his own life Joyce knew such women well – in Dublin as well as, later, on the continent. For example Hannah Sheehy, who married Francis Skeffington, was active in feminist struggles. According to J. F. Byrne, during the ten years prior to Joyce's enrollment at the university, highest honours in Modern Literature had invariably gone to a woman (55). In Paris, Joyce had been invited by Maud Gonne to call on her, but his 'shabby appearance' led him to be too proud to take advantage of her suggestion (*MBK* 198–9). For all his bravado, Joyce was fully aware of the role women could take and were taking in cultural, artistic and intellectual life, and of how limiting male attitudes could be. In Rome in 1906, while working in a bank, he reacted to the opinions of a German co-worker about what a wife should be like – 'able to cook well, to sew, to housekeep, and to play at least one musical instrument' – by remarking that 'it's very hard on me to listen to that kind of talk' (*LII* 157). One of the primary reasons for his intense admiration of Henrik Ibsen was in fact the playwright's feminism; as Joyce commented once to his friend Arthur Power:

> The purpose of *The Doll's House* . . . was the emancipation of women, which has caused the greatest revolution in our time in the most important relationship there is – that between men and women; the revolt of women against the idea that they are the mere instruments of men.
>
> [35]

Yet Joyce did have some limitations in his own reaction toward educated women: many 'men of great genius', he once claimed in the context of a discussion of William Blake's marriage, are 'not attracted to cultured and refined women', and he observed of the Blakes that 'in the early years of their life together there were discords, misunderstandings easy to understand if we keep in mind the great difference in culture and temperament that separated the young couple' (*CW* 217–18); the young man making these assertions had been with Nora Barnacle eight years.

Nora Barnacle was born in March 1884, in Galway; she was from the west of Ireland – 'my little strange-eyed Ireland!' Joyce called her (*LII* 276) – but was no less an urban creature than he. The daughter of a baker (Thomas) and a seamstress (Annie), Nora was the second child; within a few years other children were born, and probably at around the age of five Nora was sent to live with her maternal grandmother, Catherine Healy, an arrangement which for whatever reason became permanent. She ceased her schooling at the age of twelve, a common practice at that time (*N* 20–1). ('You are not, as you say, a poor uneducated girl', Joyce had to assure her [*SL* 165].) She began at that early age to work, as a porteress at the Presentation Convent (*N* 22).

By the time she met James Joyce in 1904, when she was twenty and had run away to Dublin, Nora had of course had boyfriends. The one who has posthumously become most famous is Michael (Sonny) Bodkin, a student at University College in Galway and the basis for Michael Furey, Gretta Conroy's former beau in 'The Dead'. In an interview with the Irish novelist Eilis Dillon, Maria Jolas, who knew the Joyces in Paris many years later, has described a conversation one night when:

... the subject of first love came up. And Nora said – Nora was not very loquacious as a rule in those evenings, she was inclined rather to wait for him to give the tenor of the conversation – and Nora said: 'There's nothing like it. I remember when I was a girl, and a young man fell in love with me, and he came and sang in the rain under an apple-tree outside my window, and he caught tuberculosis and died'.

Dillon: As if she had never read the story!

Jolas: Or as if *we* had never read the story.[24]

Nora's early suitors provided models not only for Gretta Conroy's but also for Molly Bloom's; Molly remembers from her youth her relationship with a young man named Mulvey – 'assuming Mulvey to be the first term of his series' (*U* 601 [17.2133]). Nora used to go out walking with William Mulvagh (pronounced and sometimes spelled 'Mulvey'), an accountant. Joyce once wrote to Stanislaus that Nora 'used to go with Mulvey (he was a Protestant). . . . She says she didn't love him and simply went to pass/the time.' The words 'she says' suggest uncertainty on Joyce's part, and in the same letter he also tells of an incident when she was sixteen; a young curate took her on his lap and 'put his hand up under her dress which was shortish. She however, *I understand*, broke away' (*LII* 72; my emphasis). Like Gabriel Conroy and Leopold Bloom, Joyce found himself intensely interested in his wife's former 'lovers' and in what she may or may not have experienced with them.

Mulvagh's Protestantism was one of the reasons why Nora's brutish uncle, Thomas Healy, forbade her from seeing him; when he caught her disobeying, he ordered her mother to leave the room and – as Joyce later reported it – 'proceeded to thrash her with a big walking-stick. She fell on the floor fainting and clinging about his knees. At this time she was nineteen! Pretty little story, eh?' (*LII* 73). Within a week, she ran away to Dublin.

The young woman Joyce met was thus independent and headstrong: she never bent her character to his preconceptions about what she 'should' be like, and to his credit he seems rarely to have wanted her to. She was a self-confident woman, with a sharp wit, and striking in appearance, with beautiful auburn hair; Joyce was immediately attracted to her. They met on Nassau Street, 10 June 1904, near Finn's Hotel, where she was working as a chambermaid (*JJ* 156). She agreed to meet him on the fourteenth, but she failed to show up, and the next day Joyce wrote her a dejected note asking for another appointment ' – if you have not forgotten me!' (*LII* 42). She had not, and they did meet – almost certainly the next evening, 16 June 1904, the date that came to be known as Bloomsday. (Among Joyce's surviving papers is a note in Nora's handwriting: 'To day 16 of June 1924 twenty years after. Will anybody remember this date' [*N* 299].)

Nora apparently shocked and exhilarated him with her open sexuality and willingness to fondle him (*LII* 232–3), but they did not yet have full sexual intercourse; their relationship was not consummated until they eloped. Within a very short time, she became enormously important to him. By 1909 he could write to her that 'you have been to my young manhood what the idea of the Blessed Virgin was to my boyhood' (*SL* 165). Yet at first he had difficulty speaking to her of 'love' – presumably the 'word known to all men' (*U* 161 [9.429–30]):

You ask me why I don't love you, but surely you must believe I am very fond of you and if to desire to possess a person wholly, to admire and honour that person deeply, and to seek to secure that person's happiness in every way is to 'love' then perhaps my affection for you is a kind of love.

[*LII* 55]

He wondered himself at his reticence: 'Why should I not call you what in my heart I continually call you? What is it that prevents me unless it be that no word is tender enough to be your name?' (*LII* 56); Gabriel Conroy remembers having written to Gretta, '*Why is it that words like these seem to me so dull and cold? Is it because there is no word tender enough to be your name?*' (*D* 214). Joyce's hesitation did not last long: his letters to her move from 'Dear Nora' to 'My dear Nora' to 'Sweetheart' to 'My dear, dear Nora' to 'Dearest Nora' to 'Carissima' to 'My dearest Nora' within two months (*SL* 24–31), and after their elopement he could write to Stanislaus that 'I admire her and I love her and I trust her' (*LII* 80).

In making his decision about what course of action to take, given his feelings for Nora, he went for advice to Byrne, who reports their conversation:

Specifically, he told me he would like to take Nora away with him; and he wanted to know whether he ought to ask her, and whether I thought she would go with him if he did. I knew what he meant, so I looked at him earnestly, and I said to him, 'Are you very fond of Nora?' 'Yes, I am', he told me simply.

'Do you love Nora?' I pressed him.

'Honestly, Byrne, there's not another girl in the world I could ever love as I do Nora.'

And I said then to James Joyce, 'Don't wait, and don't hesitate. Ask Nora, and if she agrees to go away with you, take her.'

[148]

Having been advised to do what he wanted to do, Joyce did what he would have done in any case.

He made plans to teach in Switzerland, through an agency whose advertisement he answered, and proceeded to borrow the money he would need to get him and Nora there (*JJ* 176, 178). They left 8 October 1904, seen off by Joyce's father, his sister Poppie, Stanislaus, and Aunt Josephine. Nora kept apart from them, for it was being withheld from Mr Joyce that a woman was leaving with his son (*N* 11).

Both of them were exhibiting a great deal of courage – Nora in particular. Joyce had made it clear that he did not believe in the institution of marriage, and there would be no wedding. He was profoundly and justly moved by her strength and constancy (so much in contrast to the fear and timidity of the protagonist of his story 'Eveline'): as he wrote to her before their departure, 'The fact that you can choose to stand beside me in this way in my hazardous life fills me with great pride and joy' (*LII* 53).

'I admire her and I love her and I trust her': the trust was essential. In Nora Barnacle he had found someone who would not betray that trust. His father was right when he did find out about Nora, and heard her last name: 'She'll never leave him' Mr Joyce predicted (*JJ* 156). Just two weeks before their departure, Stanislaus had worried in his diary, 'I never saw Jim manage any affair so badly as he has managed his affair with Miss Barnacle' (76). Stanislaus was wrong: Joyce managed it better than perhaps any other act of his life, and his joining his life to Nora's was perhaps the wisest decision he ever made.

When they left Dublin together, Nora Barnacle was twenty years old and James Joyce was twenty-two.

2

Standing by the Door:
The Early Work

That they may dream their dreamy dreams
I carry off their filthy streams
For I can do those things for them
Through which I lost my diadem,
Those things for which Grandmother Church
Left me severely in the lurch.
Thus I relieve their timid arses,
Perform my office of Katharsis.

'The Holy Office'[1]

[Dublin: at Sheehy's, Belvedere
Place]
Hanna Sheehy – O, there are sure to be great crowds.
Skeffington – In fact it'll be, as our friend Jocax would say, the day
of the rabblement.
Maggie Sheehy – (*declaims*) – Even now the rabblement may be
standing by the door!

Epiphany #17[2]

It is largely on faith that we regard Stephen Dedalus as an artist; in
the *Portrait* we see only one poem, his villanelle, about which perhaps the best that can be said is that its lushness is not to everyone's
taste. In *Ulysses* we see even less; the closest he comes to publishing
anything is his helping Mr Deasy get his letter about foot and mouth
disease into the newspaper. We hear nothing about Stephen's writing any short stories, much less a novel. At the same age, James Joyce
was already working on his collection of stories, *Dubliners*, had
published literary and aesthetic criticism in the *Fortnightly Review*
and elsewhere, and had begun to write his autobiographical novel
Stephen Hero.

Nor was Joyce alone in believing that his career had enormous promise; in retrospect we can be impressed by his brother's references, in his diary, to Joyce as a 'genius': 'when I say "genius", I say just the least little bit in the world more than I believe. . . . He has extraordinary moral courage – courage so great that I have hopes that he will one day become the Rousseau of Ireland' (3). Joyce's own aims may even then have been still higher, as high as were his demands on himself. By 1902 he had destroyed much of the juvenilia he had thus far written (*JJ* 80, 755).

Among the works he disposed of was *A Brilliant Career*, a play written in 1900 under the influence of Ibsen. Apparently the most striking thing about it, and just about all that has survived of the play, was its dedication:

To
My own Soul I
dedicate the first
true work of my
life.

When Joyce's father saw that, his reaction was 'Holy Paul!' (*JJ* 78). William Archer, the translator of Ibsen with whom Joyce had already corresponded, was more restrained and polite, and quite kind when Joyce sent him the play. But he was also confused: it did not take long into Joyce's brilliant career before someone was responding to his work by saying that 'if you had a symbolic purpose, I own it escapes me. It may be very good symbolism for all that – I own I am no great hand at reading hieroglyphics.' Archer was not entirely diffident, however, and while he recognised – quite sincerely, it seems – the young author's talent, he had to write that 'I cannot say that I think this play a success. For the stage, of course – the commercial stage at any rate – it is wildly impossible – no doubt you realize that' (*LII* 8).

Although few readers would now make major claims for Joyce's poetry either, for a while it was his poems that he had the least trouble publishing. They were regarded as highly promising in Dublin; no less a figure than Yeats wrote to him in 1902 that 'your technique in verse is very much better than the technique of any young Dublin man I have met during my time' (*LII* 13). There is in turn a clear Yeatsian influence in some of the earliest poems, such as one published as 'Song' in 1904 (it became 'VII' in *Chamber Music*):

My love is in a light attire
  Among the apple-trees,
Where the gay winds do most desire
  To run in companies.

There, where the gay winds stay to woo
  The young leaves as they pass,
My love goes slowly, bending to
  Her shadow on the grass;

And where the sky's a pale blue cup
  Over the laughing land,
My love goes lightly, holding up
  Her dress with dainty hand.

[*Portable Joyce* 632]

Perhaps because he felt his work too much under Yeats's shadow, Joyce came to feel doubts about his full ability as a poet. As he prepared a volume of his poems for publication in 1906, he found nearly all of them 'poor and trivial' (*LII* 182). In 1909 he confessed to Padraic Colum, 'I am not a poet'. In retrospect Colum remarks that the poems 'seem to come out of a young musician's rather than a young poet's world' (Colum 55), just as Joyce had come to feel that the collection was 'a young man's book' (he was all of twenty-five when he made that comment in 1907), although 'some of them are pretty enough to be put to music' (*LII* 219). So it is not surprising that Stanislaus's original suggestion that the volume be called *Chamber Music* was accepted (*Diary* 28). ('Chamber music', Bloom reflects in *Ulysses*: 'Could make a kind of pun on that' [232; 11.979–80]; following that advice, *Finnegans Wake* speaks of 'chambermade music' [184.4]). Arthur Symons helped Joyce place the volume with the publisher Elkin Matthews (*LII* 172), and the book came out in May 1907.

Other work besides his fiction also eventually found publication, sooner or later in one way or another. Some of his aesthetic and critical ideas, notably, became part of the fabric of *A Portrait of the Artist as a Young Man*. Joyce early evinced interest in theoretical concepts of aesthetics. He delivered a paper on no less a subject than 'Drama and Life' (an encompassing title which nevertheless does not do justice to the paper's scope) in 1900.[3] In Paris he seems to have studied aesthetics a good deal more, and more profitably, than medicine. His notebook jottings have survived, and many of them have a familiar ring to readers of Stephen's theories in *Stephen Hero* and the *Portrait*:

> Desire is the feeling which urges us to go to something and loathing is the feeling which urges us to go from something: and that art is improper which aims at exciting these feelings in us whether by comedy or by tragedy. . . .
>
> . . . There are three conditions of art: the lyrical, the epical and the dramatic. . . .
>
> Art is the human disposition of sensible or intelligible matter for an aesthetic end.
>
> [CW 143, 145]

These and the other comments in the notebook are acute and interesting, but it is also true that most of their interest derives from our awareness that they are James Joyce's, and that he attributes them to his counterpart in his fiction. We do not read Joyce's criticism with the same sense of enlightenment separate from the author's fiction that we experience with, say, the essays of Virginia Woolf or Henry James.

Joyce's concept of the epiphany may provide an exception to that generalisation. To Stephen in *Stephen Hero*, as to Joyce himself, an epiphany is a 'triviality' yet 'a sudden spiritual manifestation, whether in the vulgarity of speech or of gesture or in a memorable phase of the mind itself' (211) – a sudden illumination produced by some apparently trivial, even arbitrary cause which seems out of all logical proportion to the moment of enlightenment or vision to which it leads.[4] Stephen believes it is important 'to record these epiphanies with extreme care, seeing that they themselves are the most delicate and evanescent of moments' (211). People whose gestures or vulgarity of speech, and so on, were recorded by James Joyce were not invariably pleased. Gogarty recounts how once, in a pub, Joyce slipped out of the snug ostensibly to go to the lavatory, while Gogarty was sure that he had actually gone to write down a record of what had been said; Gogarty understandably remarks that 'to be an unwilling contributor to one of his "Epiphanies" is irritating' (*As I Was Going* 294–5).

Forty of Joyce's brief manuscripts of epiphanies survive, all of them apparently composed between 1902 and the next year or two;

we have good reason to believe that the original number of epiphanies went at least into the seventies. Some are narrative or lyrical in
character, like prose poems, while others have a dialogue form. The
resulting mixture of lyricism, drama and records of seemingly mundane trivia is fascinating: Joyce was a poet, but one with what he
called 'a grocer's assistant's mind' (*LIII* 304). The epiphanies are
interesting in themselves, but probably the most intriguing thing
about them is the way most of them – twenty-five – were eventually
used in Joyce's more extended works: thirteen in *Stephen Hero*, twelve
in the *Portrait*, four even as late as *Ulysses*, and one in *Finnegans Wake*.
Probably the most famous of the dramatic epiphanies is one that
recorded a childhood incident that appears at the start of the *Portrait*:

> [Bray: in the parlour of the house
> in Martello Terrace]
> Mr Vance – (*comes in with a stick*) . . . O, you know, he'll have to
> apologise, Mrs Joyce.
> Mrs Joyce – O yes . . . Do you hear that, Jim?
> Mr Vance – Or else – if he doesn't – the eagles'll come and pull out
> his eyes.
> Mrs Joyce – O, but I'm sure he will apologise.
> Joyce – (*under the table, to himself*)
> – Pull out his eyes,
> Apologise,
> Apologise,
> Pull out his eyes.
>
> Apologise,
> Pull out his eyes,
> Pull out his eyes,
> Apologise.[5]

One of the narrative or lyrical epiphanies appears at the end of the
Portrait, in Stephen's diary:

> The spell of arms and voices – the white arms of roads, their
> promise of close embraces and the black arms of tall ships that
> stand against the moon, their tale of distant nations. They are held
> out to say: We are alone, – come. And the voices say with them:
> We are your people. And the air is thick with their company as

they call to me their kinsman, making ready to go, shaking the wings of their exultant and terrible youth.[6]

The first epiphany evokes the sense of threat, the imposition of guilt and the withdrawal and isolation of the frightened little boy; the second epiphany, the last in the novel, provides final evidence – despite the 'promise of close embraces' – of Joyce's (and Stephen's) alienation and the call of 'distant nations': of exile and flight from Dublin.

In his 'exile' Joyce never forgot Dublin – never left it, in his memory or his imagination. In any case he never wrote about any-where else. 'Joyce always said', Italo Svevo was to recall, 'that there was only room for one novel in a man's heart . . . and that when one writes more than one, it is always the same book under different disguises.'[7] And to Adolph Hoffmeister, whom he knew in Paris in the twenties and thirties, Joyce observed that 'my work is a whole and cannot be divided by book titles': rather, from *Dubliners* on, it 'goes in a straight line of development. . . . My whole work is always *in progress*' (*PAE* 129, 131). In that comment Joyce suggests that an appropriate title for his ongoing single novel might be *Work in Progress*; an even fitter one would be *Dubliners*.

We have seen how much Joyce understood he had been influ-enced by his Jesuit education; but an even profounder force on his later art was the transfer from Clongowes to Belvedere, from the countryside to the city. During all his years at Belvedere Joyce was a walker: each day, each evening after school he would wander the streets of Dublin, and he came to know them intimately and, in his own way, lovingly. Dublin was a European capital and a cultural centre, yet it was also – especially in his youth – compact and insular enough to be knowable. He always felt that one could speak of a 'Dubliner' more accurately and meaningfully than one could say 'Londoner' or 'Parisian' (*LII* 122).

Joyce once planned to write a follow-up volume after *Dubliners*, to be called *Provincials* (*LII* 92) – about as unlikely a plan as he ever daydreamed about. In truth he hardly knew much about Ireland other than his home city; as he once confessed to Thomas McGreevy, 'This Ireland that you talk about is strange territory so far as I am concerned. Thirty miles from Dublin and I am lost' (in Dawson 309). He was and always remained an urban person. He visited the coun-tryside and resort towns through much of Europe, but he always chose to live in cities; he loved their excitement, their crowds, and their restaurants and cafés. He translated that compulsion into an artistic credo, connecting modern art with cities because they 'are of primary interest nowadays. . . . This is the period of urban domination. . . . A writer's purpose is to describe the life of his day . . . and I chose Dublin because it is the focal point of the Ireland of today, its heart-beat you may say, and to ignore that would be affectation' (in Power 97).

Joyce did not intend *Dubliners* to be seen as 'a collection of tourist impressions' (*LII* 109). In 1904, having written the first story, 'The Sisters', he wrote Constantine P. Curran (in a letter signed, incidentally, 'S.D.' for 'Stephen Daedalus') that he was planning 'a series of epicleti' – invocations, as it were: 'I call the series *Dubliners* to betray the soul of that hemiplegia or paralysis which many consider a city' (*LI* 55). On the first page of 'The Sisters' in the collection as finally published, the narrator remembers how 'every night as I gazed up at the window I said softly to myself the word *paralysis*'. Joyce repeated the word in a 1906 letter to a publisher, as he explained that his 'intention was to write a chapter of the moral history of my country and I chose Dublin for the scene because that city seemed to me the centre of paralysis' (*LII* 134).

In subsequent years it would be Joyce's boast that on the basis of his art – especially *Ulysses* – 'it will be possible to reconstruct Dublin a thousand years from now just as it was at the beginning of the twentieth century'.[8] Not quite from *Dubliners* alone, perhaps: as he himself came to feel even while still working on the stories, 'Sometimes thinking of Ireland it seems to me that I have been unnecessarily harsh. I have reproduced (in *Dubliners* at least) none of the attraction of the city for I have never felt at my ease in any city since I left it except in Paris' (*LII* 166). And Constantine Curran, who had been the recipient of Joyce's original letter about paralysis, was later to recall his reaction to the pages he read of *Stephen Hero*:

> As objective criticism of the Ireland of 1904 they seemed to me to have little validity. . . . Nothing seemed to me more inept than to qualify the focus of [Irish political, cultural and literary activity at that time] . . . as a hemiplegia or paralysis, however much one might quarrel with its exuberances or fanaticisms. That Joyce thought fit to call it so is the measure of his ardour and youthful impatience. But any discussion with him of such arbitrary asser-

tions was futile; denial or attempted rebuttal was met only with some oblique, humorous, unanswerable retort.

[Curran 54–5]

One of the sources of Joyce's insistence was his own sense of isolation from the literary movements of his time and his place (he was 'unfellowed, friendless and alone', according to 'The Holy Office' [*Portable Joyce* 659]). Those movements were in fact extraordinary: while he was composing the stories of *Dubliners*, the literary lights of Dublin included AE (George Russell), George Moore, Lady Gregory, and younger figures such as John Millington Synge, Padraic Colum and, for that matter, Gogarty. And William Butler Yeats.

Above all there was Yeats, the only one of all of them whom Joyce truly admired, with an esteem that lasted his entire life.[9] We have already seen how proud Joyce always was that he refused, while at University College, to sign the protest against the production of *The Countess Cathleen* in 1899. The two men met in 1902, when Yeats was thirty-seven, and his report is one of monumental hubris on the younger man's part; according to Yeats's account Joyce read to him some of his epiphanies but then said, when Yeats praised them:

... 'I really don't care whether you like what I am doing or not. It won't make the least difference to me. Indeed I don't know why I am reading to you.' ...

Presently he got up to go, and, as he was going out, he said, 'I am twenty. How old are you?' I told him, but I am afraid I said I was a year younger than I am. He said with a sigh, 'I thought as much. I have met you too late. You are too old.'

[*Workshop* 167, 169]

Accounts of this incident differ, and Joyce later denied that he had meant any mode of 'contempt' in his comment (*JJ* 101). According to Stanislaus, 'it is reported that at their first meeting my brother said to Yeats, "I regret that you are too old to be influenced by me"; and it seems that my brother always denied the story. To the best of my recollection it is at least substantially correct, though perhaps Jim may have phrased it somewhat differently' (*MBK* 179).

Both Lady Gregory and AE, each of them very influential in Dublin literary circles (although Russell himself was then only in his mid-thirties), were kind to the young Joyce and recognised his talent and, even more, his extraordinary personality. In Paris, he met the young John Millington Synge before any of Synge's plays had been produced; Joyce later claimed that he had been the first person to read *Riders to the Sea* (*LI* 36). In fact he was not very impressed by the play, but Synge and he got along well and had lively discussions: 'thanks be to God Synge isn't an Aristotelian. I told him part of my esthetic: he says I have a mind like Spinosa' (*LII* 35).

As if believing that no good deed should go unpunished, Joyce repaid the kind support of some of literary Dublin with an attack on all of it, in a broadside entitled 'The Holy Office' as if to connect the literary establishment with the Catholic Inquisition. The poem recognisably attacks Yeats ('But I must not accounted be/ One of that mumming company – '[10]), Lady Gregory, Synge, Gogarty, Colum, Russell, and others, until:

> . . . distantly I turn to view
> The shamblings of that motley crew,
> Those souls that hate the strength that mine has
> Steeled in the school of old Aquinas.
> Where they have crouched and crawled and prayed
> I stand, the self-doomed, unafraid,
> Unfellowed, friendless and alone,
> Indifferent as the herring-bone,
> Firm as the mountain-ridges where
> I flash my antlers on the air.[11]

Such temerity aside, in fact *Dubliners* had earlier had its origin in a suggestion by Russell that Joyce write a 'simple' story for the *Irish Homestead*. 'It is easily earned money', he assured him, 'if you can write fluently and don't mind playing to the common understanding and liking for once in a way. You can sign any name you like as a pseudonym' (*JJ* 163); when 'The Sisters' was published 13 August 1904, Joyce signed it 'Stephen Daedalus'. Surprisingly, he was able to publish two other stories – 'Eveline' and 'After the Race' – in this journal with a largely rural audience, until complaints from readers forced the editor to stop accepting Joyce's work (*JJ* 165).

Within a year, Joyce had full plans for a collected volume, elaborately structured; a letter to Stanislaus makes clear both that and the autobiographical bases of several of the stories:

The order of the stories is as follows. *The Sisters, An Encounter* and another story ['Araby'] which are stories of my childhood: *The Boarding-House, After the Race* and *Eveline*, which are stories of adolescence: *The Clay, Counterparts*, and *A Painful Case* which are stories of mature life: *Ivy Day in the Committee Room, A Mother* and the last story of the book [at that point, 'Grace'] which are stories of public life in Dublin.

[*LII* 111]

'An Encounter' derived from a day's 'miching' by Joyce and Stanislaus while they lived in North Richmond Street (Joyce would have been thirteen and Stannie eleven), during which they met 'an elderly pederast' (*MBK* 62). When he was a year younger, Joyce had gone to the actual bazaar, also called Araby, that figured in his story 'Araby'; William Fallon remembered coming across him that evening, getting off the train at Lansdowne Road:

When we reached the bazaar it was just clearing up. It was very late. I lost Joyce in the crowd, but I could see he was disheartened over something. I recall, too, that Joyce had had some difficulty for a week or so previously in extracting the money for the bazaar from his parent.

[Fallon, in *Joyce We Knew* 48]

Some of the stories of 'mature life' also had biographical origins; for example Stanislaus felt that Mr Duffy in 'A Painful Case' is 'a portrait of what my brother imagined I should become in middle age' – although he acknowledged too that Joyce had lent Mr Duffy 'some traits of his own' (*MBK* 160). Of course the last story in the collection, 'The Dead', which was also the last written (Joyce completed it in September 1907), depended a great deal on family history – most notably Nora's past. But in it he used his own experience as well, remembering parties at the home of his great-aunts (*JJ* 245); and while Mr Duffy is a portrait of what Stanislaus might have been, Gabriel Conroy seems in part a reflection on what Joyce himself might have become like, had he remained in Dublin and pursued a journalistic or teaching career.

Among the 'rules for good writing' Joyce laid down in his talks with Gogarty was 'Don't exaggerate. Tell the truth' (Gogarty, *Mourning* 48). Once he had left Dublin Joyce found it a bit more difficult to be as accurate as he passionately wanted to be, so in his pursuit for the full truth to tell he would write letters to Stanislaus with the following sorts of requests:

> Dear Stannie Please send me the information I ask you for as follows:
>
> *The Sisters*: Can a priest be buried in a habit?
>
> *Ivy Day in the Committee Room* – Are Aungier St and Wicklow in the Royal Exchange Ward? Can a municipal election take place in October?
>
> *A Painful Case* – Are the police at Sydney Parade of the *D* division? Would the city ambulance be called out to Sydney Parade for an accident? Would an accident at Sydney Parade be treated at Vincent's Hospital?
>
> *After the Race* – Are the police supplied with provisions by government or by private contracts?
>
> Kindly answer these questions as quickly as possible.
>
> (LII 109)

As Joyce claimed, he wrote *Dubliners* 'in a style of scrupulous meanness and with the conviction that he is a very bold man who dares to alter in the presentment, still more to deform, whatever he has seen and heard' (*LII* 134).

Determined honesty of such intensity did not, in those years, make it easy to get one's work published in Ireland. At first there seemed to be no real problem. He submitted the collection of stories to Grant Richards, a London publisher, in December 1905, and Richards accepted them in February 1906. Joyce then added a new story, 'Two Gallants', which produced a letter from Richards in April informing Joyce that the printer had objected to some passages. Joyce replied that he could not agree to Richards's request that he expunge or modify the story: 'I have written my book with considerable care, in spite of a hundred difficulties and in accordance with what I understand to be the classical tradition of my art. You must therefore allow me to say that your printer's opinion of it does not interest me in the least' (*LI* 60).

Unfortunately, however, given the publishing realities of the day (printers were held responsible, legally, for everything they printed), the printer's opinion did matter and could even be decisive. The result was a painfully prolonged series of negotiations and correspondence. The behaviour of the fearful publisher was shameful, even for the time; in ours the whole episode seems absurd (for example, one of the major obstacles to publication was Joyce's use of the word 'bloody'). Early in his correspondence with Richards, the exasperated Joyce, having 'come to the conclusion that I cannot write without offending people', impetuously and carelessly pointed out that 'a more subtle inquisitor' than the printer would also have denounced 'An Encounter' (*LII* 134), thereupon alerting Richards to the dangers of that story as well.

Joyce continued to defend his art, realising that for a short story 'details' can be crucial; he admitted that he longed for publication and could use the money he would earn from it, but he insisted that 'I have very little intention of prostituting whatever talent I may have to the public' (*LII* 137). In fact he did prove willing to compromise, offering to modify a number of the stories although insisting that all – including 'An Encounter' and 'Two Gallants' – would have to remain. He pleaded for understanding, telling Richards that 'I seriously believe that you will retard the course of civilisation in Ireland by preventing the Irish people from having one good look at themselves in my nicely polished looking-glass' (*LI* 64).

Finally, however, Richards decided he could not publish the book at all. Given the world of publishing in which he had to operate, his behaviour could charitably be regarded as timid rather than outrageous or malicious. A similarly generous reaction seems less in order towards George Roberts, of the Dublin firm of Maunsel and Co. *Dubliners* had been considered by a number of publishers for several years after Richards's decision when, in 1909, Roberts, whom Joyce had known in Dublin, accepted it. They signed a contract in August, but soon Roberts began to have his own misgivings; this time a central problem was Joyce's practice of referring to Dublin firms and shops by their actual names (a dispute that seems all the more ironic given the fact that nowadays businesses which still survive and are mentioned in Joyce's work invariably use their Joycean connection in their advertisements). Roberts feared the possibility of consequent libel actions, perhaps with some justice.[12] Nevertheless, his conduct as a publisher was totally unprofessional. He constantly prevaricated, delaying without being open about what he was doing and refusing to commit himself firmly either to abandoning the book or to publishing it. In 1911, after two years, the furious Joyce sent an open letter to Irish newspapers outlining the history of his efforts to publish his book, drawing special attention to a controversy that had arisen over references in 'Ivy Day in the Committee Room' to Edward

VII ('he's fond of his glass of grog and he's a bit of a rake, perhaps', and so on).[13]

Ignoring the public attack, Roberts continued to vacillate and make demands, to some of which Joyce agreed. Padraic Colum recalls his visit to Maunsel and Co. one day with Joyce in 1912, with a 'sulky' Roberts:

> And there was Joyce, the proudest man in Dublin, asking this man not to condemn a book he had put so much into, and like any struggling author asking the whip-handed publisher to give him a break. 'I will make deletions!' 'I will cut out the story!' And still, refusal, refusal!

> [Colum 64]

In August 1912 Roberts finally determined not to publish *Dubliners*, and the printer destroyed the sheets the next month. Roberts climaxed three years of disgraceful treatment by writing to Joyce that his solicitors had recommended that he proceed against Joyce 'in order to recover all costs, charges and expenses for time, labour and materials expended on the book'. He magnanimously assured Joyce that he would 'be extremely sorry to have to take proceedings against you', but 'I must ask you to make a substantial offer towards covering our loss' (*LII* 314).

He would have been better off not asking. Instead of sending money, Joyce paid him back by making Roberts the narrator of a satirical broadside, 'Gas from a Burner', which he wrote on his way home to Trieste, where he had it printed and then sent to Dublin for his brother Charles to distribute. In it Roberts warns against 'the black and sinister arts/ Of an Irish writer in foreign parts', and defends himself against the outrageous writings he has been asked to publish:

> Shite and onions! Do you think I'll print
> The name of the Wellington Monument,
> Sydney Parade and Sandymount tram,
> Downes's cakeshop and Williams's jam? . . .
> It's a wonder to me, upon my soul,
> He forgot to mention Curly's Hole.

> [*Portable Joyce* 660–1]

In a bitter example of some sort of justice, years later Padraic Colum met Roberts, who had come on hard times and was now the publisher of a 'vanity' press: 'I date my downfall from the Joyce affair', he told Colum 'ruefully and penitently' (Colum 65).

Arrogant as his broadside was, Joyce was despondent over the fate of his long years of effort on his collection of stories. It was still unpublished late in 1913 when, surprisingly, Grant Richards expressed willingness to consider it again. He then acted quickly; early in 1914, apparently feeling that society had been sufficiently prepared for *Dubliners*, he agreed to publish it, and the book came out in June. Times had changed for Joyce; as we shall see, earlier that year the serial publication of *A Portrait of the Artist as a Young Man* had begun.

The reviews of *Dubliners* were respectful but reserved; the spareness and 'scrupulous meanness' of the stories marked a technical advance, perhaps even a revolution, in the history of the short story in English, but most of the original reviewers were especially disturbed by Joyce's content and perceived attitude – or lack of attitude. The common thread running through the reviews was a troubled response to the 'morbidity', 'sordidness', and 'unpleasantness' of the stories; according to the review in *The Times Literary Supplement*, for example, '*Dubliners* may be recommended to the large class of readers to whom the drab makes an appeal, for it is admirably written'; in the *New Statesman*, Gerald Gould also praised Joyce – even calling him 'a man of genius' – but he too regretted the insistence in the volume 'upon aspects of life which are ordinarily not mentioned'.[14] For all such reservations, there was no legal trouble: the book was not censored, and no Dublin firms sued.

James Joyce was thirty-two when the book he had begun to write at twenty-two was finally published. When he completed its last and greatest story, 'The Dead', in 1907, he was twenty-five years old.

3

The Curve of an Emotion: The Years of the *Portrait*, 1904–1914

... the past assuredly implies a fluid succession of presents, the development of an entity of which our actual present is a phase only. ... [A] portrait is not an identificative paper but rather the curve of an emotion.

'A Portrait of the Artist'[1]

Joyce began the earliest versions of what was ultimately to become *A Portrait of the Artist as a Young Man* even before the first of the *Dubliners* stories. He wrote a sketch, or story, which Stanislaus suggested he call 'A Portrait of the Artist', in one day, 7 January 1904, after he heard that a new journal was being started, called *Dana*. He showed it to one of the editors, W. K. Magee (also called 'John Eglinton', as in *Ulysses*) one evening at the National Library; Magee records that he read it in Joyce's presence and then 'handed it back to him with the timid observation that I did not care to publish what was to myself incomprehensible' (*Workshop* 200). The sketch is indeed dense, and one could be forgiven for feeling that not much was lost to the world of literature when Magee turned it down (aside from Magee's chance to publish the future Great Writer); in fact the rejection gave Joyce the impetus to pursue his subject – himself – at length, in an autobiographical novel. He began, Stanislaus reports in his diary, 'half in anger, to show that in writing about himself he has a subject of more interest than their aimless discussion'. Again, it was Stanislaus who supplied his brother with his working title: *Stephen Hero* (*Diary* 12), after the unlikely name of its protagonist, Stephen Daedalus.

At least at the start the writing seems to have gone quickly, and Joyce finished the first chapter in a matter of weeks, by early February 1904 (*JJ* 148). The novel as it developed would have been, had he finished it in that form, a much longer book than the *Portrait* turned

40

out to be. But eventually he abandoned the *Stephen Hero* version – dramatically, according to one account, which reports that one day in Trieste, during an argument with Nora, he began stuffing the manuscript into a lighted stove. His sister Eileen was living with them at the time, and her daughter, who was not born until a decade later, remembered hearing how 'Mamma ran over immediately and snatched out as much as she could, but some five hundred pages had been burned. So were her hands. Next day he bought her some mittens, a collar, and a bow to match' (Delimata 45). The portions of the manuscript that survive have been published; although they deal only with Stephen's university days, they add up to a book about as long as the *Portrait*, for the earlier version was much more expansive and detailed.

Joyce began the new novel in 1907, while living in Trieste, and by late November he had finished the first chapter (*JJ* 264). He went back to a variation of the original title, one which openly if ambiguously invited comparisons between the lives of his hero and the author: *A Portrait of the Artist as a Young Man*. The first words of the novel as we now have it are justly famous; when the original readers came across them they must have perceived that the writer who could so put us into a child's world through language was an artist to conjure with:

> Once upon a time and a very good time it was there was a moocow coming down along the road and this moocow that was coming down along the road met a nicens little boy named baby tuckoo. . . .
> His father told him that story. . . .
>
> [7]

In 1931, almost a quarter of a century after he wrote those words, Joyce's father wrote him a letter:

> My dear Jim I wish you a very happy birthday and also a bright and happy New Year. I wonder do you recollect the old days in Brighton Square, when you were Babie Tuckoo, and I used to take you out in the Square and tell you all about the moo-cow that used to come down from the mountain and take little boys across?
>
> (*LIII* 212)

His son of course not only remembered but had years before let the world know that he did.

Joyce, who always insisted that he had 'very little imagination' (*SL* 225), had no qualms about associating himself with his hero/protagonist. While working on *Stephen Hero* he had a habit of signing his letters to friends like Gogarty and Curran with the name 'Stephen Daedalus' – or even 'Yours heroically, Stephen Daedalus' (*LI* 54–5). But it is essential to recognise that in the end Stephen is not Jim, and certainly not 'Sunny Jim'. Joyce amplified for his fictional purposes his portrayal of the lonely boy, the alienated adolescent, the aloof artist.

Other people depicted in that fiction could not always be happy about seeing themselves – or distortions of themselves – in what could easily seem to them the cracked looking-glass of Joyce's fiction. When the *Portrait* finally came out, his youngest sisters, Eva, Florrie, and May, were bitter about the depiction of the family (*N* 224). Friends were alert from the beginning to the dangers for them in Joyce's method; in 1905 Stanislaus reported to him that Byrne 'says he would not like to be Gogarty when you come to the Tower episode' (*LII* 103; the original plan seems to have been to take the *Portrait* at least through that incident, but of course it ended up being used for the start of *Ulysses*). One day in 1909, during a visit back to Dublin, Joyce encountered Gogarty, who tried to be friendly while Joyce – according to his own account in a letter to Stanislaus – remained distant but came to the point that seemed clearly to have been worrying his former friend:

> 'I bear you no illwill. . . . But I must write as I have felt'. He said 'I don't care a damn what you say of me so long as it is literature'. I said 'Do you mean that?' He said 'I do. Honest to Jaysus. Now will you shake hands with me at least?' I said 'I will: on that understanding'.
>
> [*LII* 231]

For his part Byrne was angry not about the depiction of himself as Cranly but about the result of his having told Joyce of a talk he had had with Father Joseph Darlington, which in the *Portrait* became the conversation that Stephen has with the Dean of Studies about lighting a fire; Byrne had great affection for Darlington and as late as 1927 complained to Joyce about his having 'abused' the anecdote: 'Joyce agreed with me, saying he was sorry he had written it as he had, and that he was sorry for certain other things he had written. So I said no more' (Byrne 35).

Joyce may have apologised for particulars, but he knew what he was doing, why he had to do it that way, and what his goals were; he never lacked for artistic ambition, just as Stephen goes out at the end of the *Portrait* to do nothing less than 'to forge in the smithy of my soul the uncreated conscience of my race' (253). During a visit to Dublin in 1912 Joyce wrote Nora that the Abbey would be presenting plays by Yeats and Synge: 'You have a right to be there because you are my bride: and I am one of the writers of this generation who are perhaps creating at last a conscience in the soul of this wretched race.' In the previous sentence of that letter he expressed hope that the publication of *Dubliners* might enable him to 'plunge into' his novel and finish it (*LII* 310–11). For he had completed the first three chapters more than four years earlier, by April 1908 (*LII* 234), but had then left the book aside. Not out of laziness: life had not been easy 'away from home and friends' (*P* 252) in 'exile'.

'Real adventures', reflects the boy in 'An Encounter', 'do not happen to people who remain at home: they must be sought abroad' (*D* 21), and in 1907 Joyce claimed in an essay that 'no one who has any self-respect stays in Ireland' (*CW* 171). In the official Joycean view, his own exile was an *escape* – indeed a 'hegira', the word used by Herbert Gorman in his authorised biography of Joyce to describe the 'flight from Dublin' (76). Even before he left for Paris in 1902, Joyce wrote to Lady Gregory of having 'been driven out of my country' (*LI* 53). Yet in looking at the situation from the outside, one might well view him as 'self exiled in upon his own ego' (*FW* 184.6–7); Joyce too, in his mellower moods, could refer to himself as 'a voluntary exile' (*LII* 84). After all it is the unusual outcast who can carry, as Joyce did in 1902, a letter of recommendation to whom it may concern from the Lord Mayor of his native city expressing 'very great hopes' that the bearer of the letter will have 'the same brilliant success that he has had at home' (*LII* 18). So in 1906 Joyce had to be 'content to recognise myself an exile: and, prophetically, a repudiated one' (*LII* 187).

It is not actually clear when Joyce began to see his exile as truly permanent; as late as 1920, while working on *Ulysses*, he told Ezra Pound that he planned to spend 'three months in Ireland in order to write *Circe* and the close of the book' (*LII* 468); he did not follow through on that plan, and in fact his last visit to Ireland was in 1912; but that was his third since the start of his 'exile' in 1904 – while Stanislaus, for example, when he left, did so for good and never returned. Joyce used to like to say, if asked when he might go back to Ireland, 'Have I ever left it?'[2] When Hanna Sheehy-Skeffington asked why he wrote only about Dublin, he replied, 'There was an English queen who said that when she died the word "Calais" would be written on her heart. "Dublin" will be found on mine' (Sheehy, in O'Connor 35).

Yet paradoxes remain: he apparently always retained his Dublin accent (Fallon, in O'Connor 55), but even after Irish independence he never gave up his British passport. It seems that after a while it was largely if uncertainly for the sake of his art that he determined never to return ('It would prevent me from writing about Dublin', he told Philippe Soupault [*JJ* 643]); but the distrust and the fear of betrayal and revenge also never left him. He said to Italo Svevo that 'it is dangerous to leave one's country, but still more dangerous to go back to it, for then your fellow-countrymen, if they can, will drive a knife into your heart.'[3]

One way for them to do that is to ignore you. For many decades the *Clongownian*, the official magazine of Clongowes Wood College, never once mentioned its famous alumnus, even when it occasionally would run a column on 'Clongownians in literature'; nor was there an obituary notice after Joyce's death. His name did not appear in the magazine until 1955, when a near contemporary of his wrote reminiscences of the school in the 1890s. The treatment was similar in the *Belvederian*: in 1924 – in other words, after *Ulysses* had made Joyce famous – a memoir by a contemporary mentioned Sheehy-Skeffington and others, but not James Joyce; a rector of Belvedere could say in the 1950s that Joyce 'has just been looked upon as one of the bad boys' (Bradley 1–2, 4); when Joyce's brother Charles died less than a week after James, he and not his famous brother was given an obituary in the magazine (*N* 478).

Others in Ireland were of course less blind, or myopic. Yeats, who began by feeling that never until he met Joyce had he 'encountered so much pretension with so little to show for it' (Magee in *Workshop* 201), believed by 1915 that he was 'a man of genius', 'the most remarkable new talent in Ireland today'; and in 1917 Yeats wrote Ezra Pound of his opinion that the *Portrait* was 'a very great book' (*LII* 354, 356, 388) – although in forwarding that praise Pound also felt he had to tell Joyce that 'Yeats has not read a novel for years' (*Pound/Joyce* 93). In 1932 Yeats and George Bernard Shaw invited Joyce to become a founding member of the Academy of Irish Letters; he declined the invitation as irrelevant to him, although he thanked Yeats for his past kindnesses (*LI* 325).

The attitude of Joyce's nation could be as complex and as para-doxical as his own. In 1922 the Irish Minister of Information, Desmond Fitzgerald, told Joyce of his intention to nominate him for the Nobel Prize (Manganiello 174); but after his death, when Nora investigated the possibility of his body being moved to Ireland, inquiries made it clear that James Joyce was not yet welcome in his native country (*N* 477–9). He was 'an Irish emigrant the wrong way out' (*FW* 190.36).

* * *

Joyce and Nora began their emigration believing that he had a teach-ing position waiting for him in Zurich, but they did not have enough funds to get them beyond Paris; so they stopped there and borrowed money for the rest of the trip from Dr Joseph Rivière, to whom Joyce had been introduced two years before through the graces of Lady Gregory (*JJ* 108, 183). In Zurich itself they had a rude shock: the Berlitz School had never heard of him or agreed to hire him, despite the information he had received from the British agent who had supposedly arranged his employment. After a week of suspense, the director of the school heard of an opportunity in Trieste, so they went there. Within a couple of hours of their arrival Joyce was in jail, having been arrested while trying to help out some English sailors accused of drunkenness; the British consul only reluctantly gained his release. Then it turned out that there was no available teaching position in the city after all (*JJ* 184–5).

Things looked bleak, but they improved when Almidano Artifoni (whose name Joyce appropriated for *Ulysses*) decided he could use a second English teacher at the new Berlitz school he was opening at Pola; Joyce and Nora moved there at the end of October 1904 (*JJ* 185). Pola (later in Yugoslavia and called Pula) was then part of the Austro-Hungarian Empire; a port city near Trieste on the Istrian peninsula that was once part of Italy, it was a site of agitation by the Irredentists, who sought to acquire for Italy lands with Italian-speak-ing peoples under other governments. Most of Joyce's teaching was of English to naval officers, and to him and Nora the city quickly came to seem 'a naval Siberia' (*LI* 57), although outside his hours of teaching he was able both to work on his aesthetic ideas and com-plete several chapters of *Stephen Hero*.

The director of the school was Alessandro Francini Bruni, four years older than Joyce; he had added his wife's name, Bruni, to his own, but Joyce always called him Francini (*PAE* 4). Years later, after the publication of *Ulysses* in 1922, Francini gave a public lecture on Joyce in Trieste; it was an odd performance, providing some interesting perspectives but ending somberly and pompously on a pious note, praying that Joyce might see the light of true faith (*PAE* 7–39). Joyce came to regard it as an unfortunate sign of what Gorman's biography, in a footnote dictated by Joyce himself on the incident, ironically refers to as 'the lasting fidelities of friendship'.[4]

But in Pola the Francinis and Joyces became very friendly, and early in 1905 the Joyces even moved into the same house, where they lived until both couples had to leave Pola. That occurred when the Austrians uncovered a spy network and expelled all foreigners from the city; the two teachers were transferred to the Berlitz school in Trieste in March 1905 (*JJ* 194).

Now in Italy but then under Austria, Trieste was a busy port with characteristics of both eastern and western Europe; the Joyces were to live there for almost ten years. At first they had difficulty finding a place to live, for Nora was pregnant, and many flats were not available to families with a baby; they had various addresses during their time in the city – including, for several months in 1906, a house they shared with the Francinis (*JJ* 215).

By then the Joyces had become parents: Nora gave birth to a baby boy in their flat 27 July 1905; after an initial telegram to Stanislaus, 'Son born Jim',[5] Joyce wrote more details. They had miscalculated the expected birth by a month, so at first when he returned from a café at three o'clock he did not know why Nora was in pain, and she had not prepared the things that would be needed: 'However, our landlady is a Jewess and gave us everything we wanted.' He summoned one of his pupils, a doctor, who arrived in time to help with the birth. Joyce delightedly reported that 'the child appears to have inherited his grandfather's and father's voices' (*LII* 100); Joyce was right about that, and both parents would come to feel pleasure and pride in their son's singing voice. The child was named Giorgio, after Joyce's brother George who had died in 1902.

Perhaps surprisingly, Joyce turned out to be a popular and effective teacher; the Italian novelist and journalist Silvio Benco, who became friends with him, remembered that in his youth 'people in Trieste began to talk of the newcomer who was a marvel at teaching English' (*PAE* 50). Joyce's success came in spite of his unorthodox approach – his methods seem to have consisted largely of conversations, and sometimes of his reading and discussing his own writing with his pupils; one mother cancelled lessons when she found both Joyce and his pupils sliding down the balustrade (*JJ* 341). Nevertheless Joyce was especially praised, he reported to Stanislaus, by 'noblemen and signori and editors and rich people', leading to concern by Artifoni that he might attempt to find a teaching position elsewhere – and to a warning to Joyce that if there were any sign of his doing so he would be fired; for Joyce the school regime was a 'reign of terror' (*LII* 94). He did however manage to do some private tutoring, and then in 1907 resigned from the Berlitz to teach privately, effectively in competition with the school. Later, in 1912, he tried to obtain a position in a public school in Italy, even taking a series of examinations administered in Padua; he passed but was subsequently informed that his Irish degree was not valid for the purposes of the Ministry of Education. But the next year he did join the Scuola Superiore di Commercio Revoltella, in Trieste, in a position which permitted him to retain his private pupils as well (*JJ* 320–1, 339).

During these years in Trieste Joyce also occasionally delivered public lectures and wrote journalism for *Il Piccolo della Sera*; many of the topics he treated were political, for he had strong views, both on general issues – he regarded himself as a socialist – and, of course, on 'the Irish question': he wrote in a 1907 article that 'there is no problem more snarled than this one. The Irish themselves understand little about it, the English even less. For other people it is a black plague' (*CW* 199). He supported independence for Ireland, but he had difficulty with nationalist fervor, especially when it became mixed with attacks on the English language and even with anti-semitism. He abhorred 'the old pap of racial hatred': 'anyone can see that if the Irish question exists', he wrote in a 1906 letter to Stanislaus, 'it exists for the Irish proletariat chiefly' (*LII* 167). He also felt that it did little good 'to fulminate against the English tyranny while the Roman tyranny occupies the palace of the soul' (*CW* 173). As such a view suggests, his views on Irish history and politics could be bitter. Years before Yeats wrote in 'September 1913' his famous refrain, 'Romantic Ireland's dead and gone,/ It's with O'Leary in the grave' (*Collected Poems* 106), Joyce used the occasion of John O'Leary's death in 1907 to say that he 'was a figure from a world which had disappeared' but one who would be publicly mourned, 'because the Irish, even though they break the hearts of those who sacrifice their lives for their native land, never fail to show great respect for the dead' (CW 191–2).

Another motif in Joyce's political writings was his hatred of violence; at the age of sixteen he had written a student essay entitled 'Force' in which he argued that 'when right is perverted to might, or more properly speaking, when justice is changed to sheer strength, a subjugation ensues – but transient not lasting' (CW 24). In *Ulysses* Leopold Bloom similarly expresses his disapproval of 'violence and intolerance in any shape or form. It never reaches anything or stops anything. . . . It's a patent absurdity on the face of it to hate people because they live round the corner and speak another vernacular, in the next house so to speak' (525 [16.1099–103]). In later years Joyce became much less public and vocal about politics, and well before that – in, for example, a 1907 letter to Stanislaus – he resisted labelling his opinions, declaring 'I have no wish to codify myself as anarchist or socialist or reactionary' (LII 217); nevertheless, as Dominic Manganiello has shown, his 'political views did not alter greatly, even after 1922' (Manganiello 174).

Early in the stay in Trieste Joyce keenly felt the absence of his 'whetstone', Stanislaus, the person 'capable of understanding me' (LII 48) and to whom Joyce wrote in 1906 that 'on all subjects – except socialism (for which you care nothing) and painting (of which I know nothing) – we have the same or like opinions' (LII 157). It could not have been easy for Stanislaus to grow up under the shadow of such an older brother. He was, as Joyce recognised, intelligent and talented, and intensely interested in many of the same things as his brother; but his writing, for example, was confined to the diary which he started in his youth and kept up all his life (although only the Dublin section has been published). He intensely admired James, but he did not idolise him; he wrote in his diary in 1904:

> My life has been modelled on Jim's example, yet when I am accused, by my unprepossessing Uncle John or by Gogarty, of imitating Jim, I can truthfully deny the charge. . . . But it is terrible to have a cleverer older brother, I get small credit for originality. I follow Jim in nearly all matters of opinion, but not all. Jim, I think, has even taken a few opinions from me. . . . *I think I may safely say I do not like Jim.* I perceive that he regards me as quite commonplace and uninteresting – he makes no attempt at disguise – and although I follow him fully in this matter of opinion, I cannot be expected to like it.
>
> [50–1]

Joyce's cynical veneer may have exaggerated the sense of his low opinion of Stanislaus; at one point he wrote his brother that he intended to dedicate *Dubliners* to him, and he clearly cared deeply about Stannie's opinions of the stories: 'Do you think they are good?' (*LII* 80).

He missed Stanislaus, his support, and his judgment. At first he casually mentioned, as early as November 1904 in Pola, that Nora had suggested to him that he help Stannie leave Ireland. By September 1905 he took the idea so seriously that he arranged for a position at the Berlitz School and spoke to his landlady about the vacant room next to his and Nora's, and worked out the best route from Dublin (*LII* 71, 112–13). For his part Stanislaus was understandably nervous but also receptive, for he longed to leave his native land perhaps even more strongly than his brother had; he wrote in his diary that the word 'Irish' 'epitomises all that is loathsome to me', and in a separate note he spoke of his loneliness: 'The interest which I took in Jim's life was the main interest I took in my own; my life is dull without him' (23, vi). So within a surprisingly short time he made his decision and left for Trieste in October 1905, Joyce having sent money for the journey by boat and train and also having arranged for him to rent the room next door. Stanislaus remained a resident of Trieste for the rest of his life.

His relationship with his brother turned out to be often strained; over the years he frequently took on – or felt himself forced to adopt – a restraining and even policing role, in light of what seemed to him Joyce's excesses and profligate ways. Stanislaus was a sober, formal, reserved burgher in essential respects (their sister's children called Joyce 'Jim', but he was always 'Uncle Stannie' [Delimata 47]). Too often his function seemed to be to rescue his brother's family from financial disaster; inevitably that duty led to frequent quarrels. Matters were not helped by his own attraction to Nora, and his pain at her indifference, although he kept such feelings secret except for recording them in the still unpublished portions of his diary (*N* 117).

Above all, however, there were the Joyces' spendthrift habits, for Stanislaus felt that his brother had 'an attitude towards money that to me, with my middle-class ideas on the subject, was like a hairshirt during all our life together' (*MBK* 231). Despite a fairly low income, Joyce and Nora dined out almost every evening, always lived at good addresses in enviable neighbourhoods, and dressed well and fashionably. As a result they were often in debt, a situation to which Joyce felt accustomed because of his father's way of life in Dublin, in an approach toward day-to-day existence that Joyce had adopted well before leaving that city. Joyce felt contempt for 'people who think that the whole duty of man consists in paying one's debts' (*LII* 100). He resisted pressures to acknowledge that duty; once, away from Nora and looking forward to his return, he wrote begging her to make him 'feel from the first moment I put my foot inside my house that I am going to be happy in every way. Don't begin to tell me stories about debts we owe' (*LII* 171). The situation did not improve, and during his years in Trieste it was almost as if he took to heart Bloom's thought in *Ulysses* that 'too much happy bores' (228 [11.810]).

Still another area of friction, with Nora as well as Stanislaus in this case, centred on Joyce's heavy drinking, a habit Stannie dated from their mother's death (*MBK* 245) but which now seemed exacerbated; in Dublin Byrne had been concerned that Joyce might become a drunkard, and in a 1907 postcard to Stannie Joyce reflected that 'a little more of this life and J.F.B.'s prophecy would be fulfilled' (*LII* 193, 214); it never was, but the habit of drinking a good deal in the evening, often so much that he had to be taken home by friends, remained. Too much alcohol also seemed to worsen some serious eye trouble he was now beginning to have, and one attack of iritis was so severe that he swore off alcohol (twice) in 1908 (*JJ* 268).

After Joyce had been at the Berlitz School for a year, it ran into financial difficulties when the subdirector embezzled some of its funds; Artifoni warned the two brothers ahead of time that the school would not be able to employ both of them during the slow summer season (*JJ* 222). Ready for a change in any case, Joyce saw an advertisement in the 11 May 1906 Rome *Tribuna* for a 'young man, twenty-five, able to speak and write perfectly French and English'. Joyce, twenty-four, responded to the ad and in the reply learned that it had been placed by a bank in the city centre, Nast-Kolb and Schumacher. During the negotiations that ensued, he took the possibility of working in a bank very seriously; he read copiously on the subject of banking, and two notebooks survive with his notes from his reading, with headings like 'Commercial Law', 'Insurance', 'Shipping', 'The Stock Exchange', and – interestingly in regard to the future creator of Leopold Bloom – 'Advertising'.[6]

Joyce was offered the position on a temporary basis and had high expectations for what it would mean for his financial and artistic well-being; he wrote in June that 'as the salary (£150 a year) is nearly double my present princely emolument and as the hours of honest labour will be fewer I hope to find time to finish my novel in Rome within a year or, at most, a year and a half' (*LII* 140). He arrived in Rome with his wife and one-year-old child 31 July 1906. His hopes for a great deal of time for his own work were soon dashed; the firm had a policy against 'extra jobs', but Joyce had to ignore it and began giving private lessons in English (Onorati, in Melchiori 26). He quickly took a profound dislike to the entire city, which reminded him 'of a man who lives by exhibiting to travellers his grandmother's corpse'. Even the art struck him as not much more than illustrations for 'a page or so of the New Testament' (*LII* 165, 201). Choosing to live in the city that provided the home of the Catholic Church he had so virulently rejected does seem a fascinating decision for him to have made. He was not comfortable there, and on top of that his writing was not going well; he could not work on his novel – or on anything else. He did have one promising idea for a story for *Dubliners*; it would be about a Mr Hunter he had known in Dublin, but in February 1907 he had to confess to Stanislaus that *'Ulysses* never got forrader than the title'; two weeks later he wrote him that 'my mouth is full of decayed teeth and my soul of decayed ambitions', and in March he lamented that 'to continue as I am at present would certainly mean my mental extinction. It is months since I have written a line and even reading tires me' (*LII* 209, 216–17). The lament echoes that of Little Chandler in 'A Little Cloud', which Joyce had already written the previous year: 'It was useless. He couldn't read. He couldn't do anything. The wailing of the child pierced the drum of his ear. It was useless, useless! He was a prisoner for life' (*D* 84).

Joyce gave notice to the bank and asked for his old job at the Berlitz School in Trieste; he was turned down, unsuccessfully looked for a job elsewhere in Europe and finally decided to return to Trieste in any case and take his chances teaching privately. He left 7 March; two evenings earlier he had been robbed of his last salary and severance pay after a drinking bout (Melchiori 22). In *Exiles*, it will be Rome in which Richard Rowan has spent his nine years of exile.

Prospects in Trieste were not good, although Joyce did resume teaching private pupils; tensions over money reached a point where, in 1909, Stanislaus left to live on his own. Meanwhile Joyce supplemented his income with some journalism and public lectures.

He needed money more than ever. In July 1907 he was hospitalised for rheumatic fever; he was still in the hospital when, on 26 July, Nora gave birth to their second child, a daughter, to whom they gave the middle name of Anna, after Nora's mother Annie, and the first name of Lucia, after the patron saint of light and eyesight. The latter name may have come to seem ironic, given the fact that the child had a cast in one eye which gave her a squint about which her parents were concerned and which caused her, later, to worry about its effect on her appearance (*N* 112–13). The next year, in August 1908, Nora had a miscarriage after a pregnancy of three months (*JJ* 268).

In 1909 Joyce determined that it was time for him to return to Dublin for a visit; for one thing, he wanted to arrange with George Roberts and Maunsel and Co. for the publication of *Dubliners*; for another, Joyce the 'exile' thought of looking into the possibility of obtaining a teaching position at the university; and he wished his father to see Giorgio, who turned four during their journey to Ireland. Nora and Lucia stayed in Trieste.

If, as has been suggested, Joyce was acting the return of Gallaher of 'A Little Cloud' for 'the benefit of the impressionable Little Chandlers' (Cixous 531), his role must have been difficult to carry off, for during the five years he had been away a number of his university friends had prospered: Gogarty was a surgeon, Curran a lawyer, and Thomas Kettle a member of Parliament engaged to Mary Sheehy, upon whom Joyce had once had a crush (*N* 126). Gogarty tried to be friendly, and invited him to Enniskerry to meet his wife, but Joyce declined, reporting to Stannie that 'he offered me grog, wine, coffee, tea: but I took nothing' (*LII* 231). (As Stephen Dedalus has learned from the Count of Monte Cristo, one does not dine in the house of one's enemy: 'Madam, I never eat muscatel grapes' [*P* 63].) Joyce did spend a pleasant afternoon at Byrne's home at 7 Eccles Street, bringing Giorgio with him 'in beaming pride' (Byrne 155).

The most fateful meeting was with Vincent Cosgrave, who was not doing so well in the world. Cosgrave, who had tried to steal Nora from Joyce five years before, had been annoyed by the name chosen for his counterpart in *Stephen Hero* (a name infamous in Irish history and legend as that of a man who hanged his own son): 'why in the name of J. – Lynch?' he wrote Joyce, 'Anything but that' (*JJ* 205). Bitterly, now, he told Joyce one day in August that on the evenings when Joyce had believed Nora could not go out with him because she was working at Finn's, she was really with Cosgrave. The effect on Joyce was devastating; 'tortured by memories', he immediately wrote to her of his 'dead love': 'You stood with him: he put his arm round you and you lifted your face and kissed him. What else did you do together? And the next night you met *me*!'

(*LII* 232). A day later he wrote her again, no less distraught, asking if Giorgio was really his son, and pursuing his questions about what she had done with Cosgrave: 'were you lying down when you kissed? Did you place your hand on him as you did on me in the dark and did you say to him as you did to me "What is it, dear?"' (*SL* 158–9).

Nearly crazed, Joyce luckily went to Byrne and confided in him; in his memoir, Byrne, writing only two years after Nora's death, does not reveal the cause of Joyce's dismay, but he relates:

> I had always known that Joyce was highly emotional, but I had never before this afternoon seen anything to approach the frightening condition that convulsed him. He wept and groaned and gesticulated in futile impotence as he sobbed out to me the thing that had occurred. Never in my life have I seen a human being more shattered. . . . I spoke to him and succeeded in quieting him. . . . He stayed for dinner and supper and spent the night in my house. The following morning he was up early, fully out of the gloom, and after breakfast he went off, humming as he went.
>
> [Byrne 156]

What Byrne had done was simply tell Joyce that Cosgrave's story was a 'blasted lie'; in the strange letter in which Joyce reported that, he asked Nora to forgive him for his 'contemptible conduct', begged her not to read over the 'horrible letters' he had written when he was out of his 'mind with rage', yet pleaded still for 'a word of denial' – and mentioned merely in passing that he had that day signed a contract for the publication of *Dubliners* (*LII* 235). Two days later he asked her to be patient with him, confessing that he was 'absurdly jealous of the past' (*LII* 237).

Nora, meanwhile, had shown Joyce's letters to Stanislaus, who then revealed that Cosgrave had told him that he had tried unsuccessfully to take Nora from Joyce but had sworn Stanislaus to secrecy (*JJ* 281). We cannot be sure of the full truth behind the whole episode; Nora seems at least to have known Cosgrave well enough to identify who the unnamed 'friend' mentioned in Joyce's letters was, but we should no doubt recall that in any case at the time of those walks by the Dodder neither Joyce nor Nora had fully committed themselves to each other.[7] Whatever had happened or had not between Cosgrave and Nora before she pledged herself to him, Joyce was mistaken about his wife's untrustworthiness, and he knew it –

except insofar as 'a man of genius makes no mistakes. His errors are volitional and are the portals of discovery' (*U* 156; 9.228–9).

Other aspects of the stay in Dublin were also souring him; the possibility of an appointment at the university came to nothing, and although he had reached an agreement with Maunsel and Co. in regard to *Dubliners*, he now felt more than ever 'sick, sick, sick . . . of Dublin! It is the city of failure, of rancour and of unhappiness' (*LII* 239). He had in his frenzy decided not to take a planned trip with Giorgio to see Nora's family in Galway, but now he went and had a good visit with the Barnacles and liked Nora's mother very much (*LII* 240).

Before going back to Trieste, Joyce decided to bring a part of his family and of Ireland with him. He had been disturbed at the plight of his sisters with only their father to care for them, so one of them, he felt, should come with him (*JJ* 285). It was decided that it should be Eva; not yet eighteen, she left with Joyce and Giorgio when they returned home to Trieste in September.

Hardly were they back when Joyce found a reason to return again. Eva, not otherwise enamoured of her new city, did like its cinemas, and wondered aloud why Dublin did not have even one (in a year when the number of cinemas in the United States alone, for example, reached 10 000 [Daniel 120]). Inspired, Joyce proposed to a group of Trieste businessmen that he undertake to start a cinema in Dublin, with their backing; they agreed, and he left for Ireland in mid-October. By the end of the month he had located a building for Dublin's first cinema, to be called the Volta, and two of his 'partners' arrived there the next month (*JJ* 300–1).

The letters to Nora from this period are among the most dramatic and fascinating of all those Joyce ever wrote. There had apparently been some friction between them, and she may even have threatened to leave him (*LII* 265). Nora's life was difficult in many ways; it had been especially harsh on their arrival in Trieste, when she keenly felt her inadequacy with the local dialect; Joyce reported in 1905 that 'girls and women are so rude to Nora that she is afraid to go out in the street'; later in the same long, rambling letter to Stannie he recounted that Nora had warned him that she could not take much longer the life they were leading (*LII* 93, 95). For his part Joyce admired her courage in facing the difficulties of her strange new life with her unusual, often impractical husband, but for a brief time he nevertheless thought of leaving her. He wrote to his Aunt Josephine hinting as much, confessing to her late in 1905:

It is possible that I am partly to blame if such a change as I think I foresee takes place but it will hardly take place through my fault alone. I daresay I am a difficult person for any woman to put up with but on the other hand I have no intention of changing. . . . I am not sure that the thousands of households which are with difficulty held together by memories of dead sentiments have much right to reproach me with inhumanity.

[*LII* 128–9]

But as the years went by he came to love and respect Nora more than ever. During the first return visit to Dublin he told her, 'You have been to my young manhood what the idea of the Blessed Virgin was to my boyhood'; during his second he wrote, 'My love for you is really a kind of adoration' (*LII* 242, 257). He might try occasionally to transform her and teach her; on a subsequent trip to Dublin in 1912 he wrote asking her, 'will you read if I give you books? Then we could speak together. Nobody loves you as I do and I should love to read the different poets and dramatists and novelists with you as your guide' (*LII* 310). But he came more and more to cherish and depend on the woman she was, not the one he would sometimes imagine she might become, and it was the real Nora who was increasingly central to his art; by the second Dublin trip in 1909 he could tell her of his certainty 'that if I am to write anything fine or noble in the future I shall do so only by listening at the doors of your heart' (*LII* 254).

Joyce fully realised the importance of sexuality within his feelings of love, devotion and adoration for Nora. He was convinced that claims of pure spiritual love are cant; as he wrote to Stannie in 1906:

. . . my opinion is that if I put down a bucket into my own soul's well, sexual department, I draw up Griffith's and Ibsen's and Skeffington's and [Father] Bernard Vaughan's and St. Aloysius' and Shelley's and Renan's water along with my own. And I am going to do that in my novel (inter alia) and plank the bucket down before the shades and substances above mentioned to see how they like it: and if they don't like it I can't help them. I am nauseated by their lying drivel about pure men and pure women and spiritual love and love for ever: blatant lying in the face of the truth.

[*LII* 191–2]

In 1909 the importance to Joyce of sexuality was reflected in a series of vigorously erotic and emotionally powerful letters to his wife.

One purpose of the sensuous correspondence was masturbatory: he urged her to write in such a way as to enable him to rouse himself to masturbation, and although her letters have apparently not survived, she clearly cooperated and succeeded; he worried that he was being so successful in his own letters that 'I was afraid, Nora, you might get so hot that you would give yourself to somebody' (*SL* 184–7). The explicit language and imagery of the letters are even more notable because Joyce, for all his later fame as the author of the 'dirty' book *Ulysses*, was in his social life reticent about the 'soul's well, sexual department'; as he reminded Nora, truthfully: 'dearest, I never use obscene phrases in speaking. You have never heard me, have you, utter an unfit word before others. When men tell in my presence here filthy or lecherous stories I hardly smile' (*SL* 182). Within the 1909 letters, however, he used language he knew would ordinarily be seen as shocking, and indulged in fantasies that would be regarded as even more so (for example of Nora flogging him); he wrote elaborately of his fascination with her undergarments, and lustfully described how he and Nora would make love on his return to Trieste; some details of his description look toward H. G. Wells's claim, upon reading the *Portrait*, that Joyce had a 'cloacal obsession' – an observation about which Joyce would remark, 'How right Wells was'.[8]

The correspondence still has the power to shock, and sometimes to disturb. What is too often passed over about the erotic love letters to Nora is that they are *love* letters. They vividly reveal his physical desire and passion – and, too, his deep emotional need and dependence. Above all they reveal his profound love.

The Volta opened on 20 December; a few more items of business had to be taken care of, and on 2 January 1910 Joyce left Dublin – again with one of his sisters, this time Eileen, who would be twenty-one in three weeks. Eileen was both older and more independent than Eva, who could not feel comfortable as an expatriate and returned to Ireland in 1911. Eileen married Frantisek Schaurek, a Czech who worked for a bank in Trieste, April 1915; they gave their first daughter, born 1917, the name Bozena (Beatrice) Berta, after the two chief women in Joyce's *Exiles*.[9] Back in Dublin, without Joyce or any native Irish person to supervise it, the Volta failed to break even and was sold by the end of the summer (*JJ* 311).

The strain of teaching was relieved to an extent by Joyce's relationship with one or two notable pupils. Ettore Schmitz was more than twenty years older than Joyce, a well-to-do manager of an industrial paint company. He had been less successful as an author, having written two novels, *Una Vita* and *Senilità* (later translated as *A Life* and *As a Man Grows Older*), which had been ignored; discouraged, Schmitz – who published and eventually became well known under the pseudonym Italo Svevo – had given up writing. One day in 1907 Joyce read his story 'The Dead' to Svevo and his wife Livia. At some point Svevo mentioned his own novels, and Joyce took them home to read, wondering what he might make of them – and was genuinely impressed (Furbank 81–2). Svevo was so moved by Joyce's sincere praise that he took up writing seriously again and went on to write some of his most admired work. It is touching to contemplate the effect of the young foreigner on the middle-aged businessman, especially given the significant differences in their temperaments. Svevo's biographer writes that 'as personalities Joyce and Svevo complemented each other in a number of ways – Svevo outwardly the perfect bourgeois, urbane, ironic and pessimistic; and Joyce, young, restless, arrogant, flamboyantly bohemian' (Furbank 83). But there were barriers of social and economic class as well, which kept their relationships quite formal; Joyce later recalled that he was never invited to the home of Svevo and his wife socially and crossed their threshold only 'as a paid teacher', and that Signora Schmitz would become 'longsighted when she met Nora in the street' (*LIII* 241).

In the mid-1920s, however, after Svevo's *La coscienza di Zeno* (*The Confessions of Zeno*) was published in 1923, Joyce – who regarded it as Svevo's finest work – helped to bring attention to it in Paris. One result was a new edition of *Senilità*, in the preface of which Svevo expressed his gratitude for Joyce's 'goodness of heart', 'generosity' and 'greatness of spirit' (Furbank 137–8). Joyce may have felt more than compensated; for one thing, as he told Svevo, he adopted Livia Schmitz's first name and long flowing hair for Anna Livia Plurabelle in *Finnegans Wake* (*LIII* 211–12). He had already borrowed some aspects of the character of his sensitive businessman friend for Leopold Bloom. In particular, Svevo was Jewish, more or less (like Bloom, more or less): his parents were 'practising Jews, of a not very strict kind', while his wife's father was also Jewish (Furbank 6, 38). Joyce learned a good deal about Jewish traditions and customs from the answers to the questions with which he plied Svevo during the years in Trieste during which he worked on *Ulysses*.

We have already seen Joyce's impatience with anti-semitism. In 1904, a relatively rare but bitter Irish example of it had surfaced in Limerick when a priest, Father John Creagh, accused Jews of violence against Christians and of desiring to 'kidnap and slay Christian children'; he initiated a boycott and other forms of agitation (such as telling gentiles that they need not honour debts to Jews) which led to the financial ruin and emigration of about half the small Jewish community in Limerick, before his Church superiors disowned his beliefs and removed him from the city (Hyman 212–17). In *Ulysses* Mr Deasy claims that Ireland 'has the honour of being the only country which never persecuted the jews' because 'she never let them in' (30 [2.437–8, 446]). Deasy is wrong, of course; Ireland had let them in. His other claim, that the Jews never suffered persecution in Ireland, was often expressed; for example, in 1888 the Mayor of Cork wrote to a newspaper that 'Irishmen are proud of the fact that theirs is the only country in Europe in which Jews have never been persecuted' (quoted in Hyman 220); the actual record is less perfect than that, although not particularly dishonourable by the standards of most European history.

Interestingly, Joyce's high regard for Jews – for example he claimed to Budgen that 'they are better husbands than we are, better fathers and better sons' – was reciprocated in his native land; in the 1930s when Samuel Beckett replied to his question as to whether anyone in Dublin read *Ulysses* by naming various people, Joyce was struck: 'But they're all Jews', he realised (quoted in *JJ* 373, 702).

Two other Jewish students in Trieste were women to whom Joyce may have been attracted. Richard Ellmann believes that the woman with whom the speaker is infatuated in *Giacomo Joyce* was probably Amalia Popper (the daughter of a Jewish businessman named Leopoldo, incidentally), whom Joyce knew between 1911 and 1914, but admits that the identification cannot be certain (*JJ* 342). Much earlier, in 1905, Brenda Maddox believes, Joyce carried on a flirtation with an Anny Schleimer, whose banker father cut off her lessons (*N* 89–90).

Svevo helped Joyce out in 1912 by agreeing to pay in advance for twelve English lessons (*JJ* 322): Joyce needed the money because Nora had gone to Ireland with Lucia, to see her family in Galway; she was supposed to get money from her uncle to send to Joyce so he and Giorgio could join them. But when she did not immediately write, Joyce decided that he and his son must go at once. He first dashed off a letter to her in which he said he could 'neither sleep nor think', and that during the night he had wakened Giorgio 'three times for fear of being alone'. Actually, Nora had already written a letter describing how 'dreadfully lonely' she was without him (*LII* 296, 297), but by the time it arrived he had left.

He stopped off in London, where he saw Yeats, and then in Dublin, where he attempted to negotiate with Roberts about the publication of *Dubliners*, before going on to Galway. There he wrote his poem 'She Weeps over Rahoon', inspired by the cemetery at Rahoon, with its grave of Michael Bodkin (the original for Michael Furey in 'The Dead'): 'Rain on Rahoon falls softly, softly falling,/ Where my dark lover lies' (*Portable Joyce* 650).

Joyce went back to Dublin, and another poem came out of the Irish trip: 'Gas from a Burner', the result of the crisis with Roberts we have seen in Chapter 2. Joyce left Dublin in September and never returned to Ireland again.

In December 1913, only a few weeks after Grant Richards decided to reconsider the possibility of publishing *Dubliners*, Joyce received a letter from a man who introduced himself as someone to whom Yeats had spoken about Joyce's writing; the stranger, an American named Ezra Pound, said that he was connected with a journal called *The Egoist* and hoped that Joyce might have something appropriate for publication in it. At the end of his letter he added in longhand, 'From what W.B.Y. says I imagine we have a hate or two in common – but thats a very problematical bond on introduction' (Pound 18). Pound, a few years younger than Joyce, had by then published several volumes of poetry and was even more active, it seemed, as an editor; the following year he would edit the influential *Des Imagistes: An Anthology* and also help Wyndham Lewis to prepare *Blast*, the Vorticist review. Joyce must have been delighted by this invitation that came out of nowhere, but he could not have foreseen how important the connection with Pound would be for his career.

Joyce sent Pound *Dubliners* and the first chapter of the *Portrait*, and in mid-January 1914 Pound excitedly replied that 'your novel is damn fine stuff. . . . Confound it, I can't usually read prose at all not anybody's in English except James and Hudson and a little Conrad' (Pound 24). *The Egoist*, for a time edited by Dora Marsden, had begun as *The New Freewoman*, but Pound had become involved with it and had urged a new name. A number of literary figures who went on to achieve distinction were connected to it one way or another, notably Rebecca West, Richard Aldington, H. D., and T. S. Eliot. Marsden's co-founder, Harriet Shaw Weaver, became editor in 1914, in time to oversee the completion of the serial publication of *A Portrait of the Artist as a Young Man*. That serialisation began, auspiciously, on Joyce's birthday, 2 February 1914. (*Dubliners* would come out in June of that year.) Joyce had almost entirely abandoned working on his novel since 1908, but he was spurred to write the fourth and fifth chapters as the first portions were appearing.

Joyce would later say that Pound 'took me out of the gutter' (Colum 66); although hyperbolic, the remark gives a hint of the significance of their relationship. Pound's own career was one of tragi-comic villainy in the 1930s and 1940s and of pathos in his last decades; but in his late twenties and early thirties his championship of Joyce and other writers, particularly Eliot, was impassioned and unselfish, even heroic. Once having secured the serial publication of a first novel by a writer whom he had never met, he proceeded to do what he could to bring about its publication in book form. By the time its serial publication was completed on 15 September 1915, the *Portrait* had been rejected by two book publishers, and by a third the following month. In January 1916 the firm of Duckworth and Co. forwarded to James B. Pinker, who had become Joyce's literary agent – he was already Joseph Conrad's – the reader's report on the novel by Edward Garnett. He recognised some of its strengths – 'ably written', he called it – but stressed that 'it is too discursive, formless, unrestrained, and ugly things, ugly words, are too prominent', and he added that 'it is too "unconventional"' (Pound 64).

When we realise that Garnett was a sensitive and intelligent reader who enthusiastically championed such new writers as D. H. Lawrence, Virginia Woolf (he praised the manuscripts of both *Sons and Lovers* and *The Voyage Out*), John Galsworthy, and Dorothy Richardson, and who was close to Joseph Conrad, his reaction reveals all the more forcefully how new, how different, *A Portrait of the Artist* truly was. Pound's response was not a patient one, however: he wrote to Pinker, 'I most emphatically will not forward the insults of an imbecile to one of the very few men for whom I have the faintest respect' and said that 'altering Joyce to suit Duckworth's reader' would be like trying to 'fit the Venus de Milo into a piss-pot – a few changes required' (Pound 67).

Harriet Shaw Weaver proposed that *The Egoist* bring out the book as well; a remaining problem was the same as it had been for *Dubliners*: the reluctance of printers. Installments of the *Portrait* had already been censored, despite Weaver's objections, in issues of *The Egoist*; sentences containing the word 'ballocks' or referring to farting had been deleted by the printers (*DMW* 103). Various printers wrote explanations, all of a piece, for their refusals to take on the novel: 'we are convinced that you would run a very great risk in putting such a book on the market'; 'it contains objectionable matter which we could not print'; 'we cannot proceed . . . unless the passages marked in blue pencil are modified or removed'; and so on (Gorman 235–6). Finally an American publisher, B. W. Huebsch, agreed to bring out the novel; it appeared in the United States 29 December 1916.[10] Weaver used sheets printed in the States for the English edition, which came out 12 February 1917.

It was an active time. Joyce had begun to write a new novel, *Ulysses*, and had completed his only play, *Exiles*, for which he had made notes late in 1913. The play's presentation of the relationship between an exiled author and his wife clearly reflects aspects of his life with Nora, and the treacherous friend, Robert Hand, draws upon Cosgrave, Gogarty, and an Italian friend, Roberto Prezioso, editor of the newspaper for which Joyce occasionally wrote, *Il Piccolo della Sera*; Prezioso had attempted to become Nora's lover (*JJ* 316–17). Reactions to the play and opinions of its success as drama have always been mixed, and Joyce was disappointed that it took so long for it to be produced; Yeats turned it down for the Abbey, and its premiere, in German translation in Munich in 1919, was not a success (*JJ* 462); *Exiles* was published in 1918 by Grant Richards.

But in the meantime Joyce was becoming widely respected as a novelist. While many critics were beginning even to speak of Joyce's 'genius', at this time perhaps no one – except Joyce, of course – believed so firmly in the appropriateness of that term as Harriet Shaw Weaver, one of the great presences in James Joyce's life. Almost six years older than he (she was born in 1876), she came from a wealthy family but had early come to the conclusion, according to her biographers, 'that her money, tainted by usury, was hers in trust' (*DMW* 87). In her thirties she became an activist in feminist causes, especially women's suffrage, and subscribed to a new periodical called *The Freewoman*. When it ran into financial trouble and appealed to readers for support, she was one of those who responded, and thus began a lifelong friendship with the journal's editor, Dora Marsden. The two women founded a subsequent periodical, *The New Freewoman*, later *The Egoist*; when its serialisation of the *Portrait* was threatened by a financial crisis, Weaver increased her subsidy

(*DMW* 87); she became sole editor in June 1914, while Joyce's novel was continuing its run, and her gifts – always anonymous – continued. Her selfless generosity, as we shall see, extended to the author too, sometimes in odd, hidden ways: before its last issue appeared in late 1919, *The Egoist* had published five installments of *Ulysses*; the records indicate that the earnings of the Egoist Press were £1637 net; Joyce's royalties were £1636 (*DMW* 234).

The response to the publication of the *Portrait* must have been immensely gratifying; it received a great deal of attention, especially for a first novel. Pound had fun compiling for publication in *The Egoist* excerpts from some of the more negative or confused reviews (for example, 'it is very difficult to know quite what to say about this new book', or 'the irreverent treatment of religion in the story must be condemned' [Pound 118, 120]). It is true that a number of reviewers could not stomach either Joyce's method or his world – or warned, as did the *Irish Book Lover*, that 'no clean-minded person could possibly allow it to remain within reach of his wife, his sons or daughters'. Irish reviews were in fact the exception; the anonymous reviewer in the *Freeman's Journal* lamented that 'English critics . . . are already hailing the author as a typical Irishman, and his book as a faithful picture of Irish life'. On the other hand Ernest Boyd, in his 1923 revision of a book originally published in 1916, *Ireland's Literary Renaissance*, would write that 'the simple truth is that *A Portrait of the Artist as a Young Man* is to the Irish novel what *The Wanderings of Oisin* was to Irish poetry and *The Playboy of the Western World* to Irish drama, the unique and significant work which lifts the *genre* out of the commonplace into the national literature'.[11] Generally most of even the first reviewers and critics were excited and impressed, and many recognised that here was a major new author.

He was thirty-three years old.

Fig. 1. George Clancy, J. F. Byrne, Joyce, while students at University College, Dublin.

Fig. 2. Students and faculty at UCD, c. 1900. Joyce is second from left, back row. Constantine P. Curran is last on the right, front row.

Fig. 3. Joyce in 1904, photographed by C.P. Curran. Asked what his thoughts were while posing, Joyce said 'I was wondering would he lend me five shillings.'

Fig. 4. Aunt Josephine Murray and three daughters.

Fig. 5. Stanislaus Joyce, c. 1905.

Fig. 6. Unidentified photo-graph taken by R.W. Simmons, Galway; possibly of Nora Bar-nacle.

Fig. 7. Eva, Joyce's sister, with
Lucia Joyce, in Trieste, c. 1910.

Fig. 8. Joyce, Zurich, c. 1918.

Fig. 9. Nora Joyce, in costume for her
role in Synge's *Riders to the Sea*,
Zurich, 1918.

Fig. 10. Sylvia Beach and James Joyce in Shakespeare and Company, 1922.

Fig. 11. Lucia Joyce, Paris.

Fig. 12. Ford Madox Ford, Joyce, Ezra Pound, John Quinn in Paris, 1923.

Fig. 13. James Joyce, Nora, Lucia, Giorgio, in Paris, 1924.

Fig. 14. Joyce with unidentified companion, probably in London, c. 1930.

Fig. 15. Joyce, his son Giorgio and grandson Stephen James, with portrait of Joyce's father John Stanislaus by Patrick Tuohy.

✝

Pray for the soul of

James A Joyce

who died at
Zurich
12th January, 1941
On whose soul sweet
Jesus have mercy
R.I.P.

Fig. 16. Card sent by Joyce's sister "Poppie" upon his death, from her convent. The date should be 13th January.

4

A Touch of the Artist: The Years of *Ulysses*, 1914–1922

As for Joyce, he treated people invariably as his equals, whether they were writers, children, waiters, princesses, or charladies. What anybody had to say interested him; he told me that he had never met a bore.

Sylvia Beach

Jim says that he writes well because when he writes his mind is as nearly normal as possible. . . .

Stanislaus Joyce

He's not one of your common or garden . . . you know . . . There's a touch of the artist about old Bloom.

Ulysses[1]

In *Ulysses*, the Blooms live at 7 Eccles Street. Joyce came to know the address because he visited J. F. Byrne there, notably on that afternoon and evening, into the night, when Byrne had reassured him about Nora's loyalty and Cosgrave's 'blasted lie'; Byrne lived in the house from 1908 to 1910, with two female cousins. Shortly before Joyce left Dublin in 1909, he visited the house once again, and he and Byrne took a long walk through the streets of Dublin. At one corner, they weighed themselves in a penny weighing machine and then walked back to Eccles Street – where Byrne discovered that his key was in his other trousers, up in his bedroom. Unperturbed, and not wanting to disturb his cousins, he climbed over the area railing, dropped down to the basement level and opened an unlocked door. Byrne was five feet, nine-and-a-half inches tall, and his weight according to the machine was eleven stone and four pounds (that is, 158 pounds), precisely the height and weight of Leopold Bloom, who had – in Joyce's fictional world – lived in the house a few years before Byrne moved in.[2] (Fortunately, no one 'really' lived there in June 1904, so Joyce could feel free to use it for the Blooms' address.)

Joyce did not actually begin writing *Ulysses* until 1914, but even before 1909 he planned to expand his original idea for a short story called 'Ulysses' into a book – 'a short book', according to Stanislaus.[3] As plans for the novel developed, not only the short story but also the *Portrait* underwent changes; for example, Joyce changed his mind about including the Martello Tower episode at the end of the one book and placed it at the start of the other.

The new novel became increasingly complicated; as Joyce reported to Pound, 'I am doing it, as Aristotle would say, by different means in different parts' (*SL* 225). Of course much of its basic structure was modelled on that of the *Odyssey*. From the time of his boyhood Joyce had been fascinated by the figure of Ulysses, about whom – at Belvedere – he had chosen to write in an essay on 'My Favourite Hero', in what was apparently regarded as an offbeat choice as distinct from the more militantly combative and less crafty Greek warriors he might have selected.[4] In adulthood too, his friends were struck by his insistence – for example in conversation with Georges Borach – that he found 'the subject of Odysseus the most human in world literature' (*PAE* 70). What Joyce meant by that is in part indicated by the question he once asked Frank Budgen: who is the most 'complete all-round character presented by any writer?' Budgen naturally guessed that Joyce was thinking of Ulysses, and Joyce went on to explain why: 'No-age Faust isn't a man. . . . Hamlet is a human being, but he is a son only. Ulysses is son to Laertes, but he is father to Telemachus, husband to Penelope, lover of Calypso, companion in arms of the Greek warriors around Troy and King of Ithaca' (*Making* 15–16).

The epic of Odysseus would have its counterpart, in the twentieth century, in a new kind of epic; as Joyce wrote to Carlo Linati, to whom he sent his detailed 'schema' for the novel:

> It is an epic of two races (Israelite – Irish) and at the same time the cycle of the human body as well as a little story of a day (life). . . . It is also an encyclopaedia. . . . Each adventure (that is, every hour, every organ, every art being interconnected and interrelated in the structural scheme of the whole) should not only condition but even create its own technique.
>
> [*LI* 146–7]

Joyce was obsessed with the need for his 'encyclopaedia' to be accurate, even in the most mundane details. He had an astonishingly precise memory in regard to the Dublin of his youth, but he would not trust it entirely. He pored over his copy of *Thom's Directory* of the city for 1904 (where, by the way, we can see that 7 Eccles Street is vacant), read over newspapers for June of that year, and bombarded friends and relatives for information that could only be conveniently found within the city, or first hand.

A special victim was Aunt Josephine. While working on the Nausicaa chapter, Joyce wrote asking her to send him novelettes and hymn books, and to answer such questions as whether any trees behind the Star of the Sea Church can be seen from the strand, and whether there are steps down to the strand from Leahy's Terrace (*LI* 135). For the Ithaca and Penelope chapters, in 1921 (twelve years after his walk with Byrne), he wrote her:

> Two more questions. Is it possible for an ordinary person to climb over the area railings of no 7 Eccles street, either from the path or the steps, lower himself from the lowest part of the railings till his feet are within 2 feet or 3 of the ground and drop unhurt. I saw it done myself but by a man of rather athletic build. I require this information in detail in order to determine the wording of a paragraph. Secondly. Do you know anything of Mat Dillon's daughter Mamy who was in Spain? If so, please let me know. Did any of your girlfriends ever go there? Thirdly and last. Do you remember the cold February of 1893. I think you were in Clanbrassil street. I want to know whether the canal was frozen and if there was any skating. Kind regards. . . .
>
> [*LI* 175]

Even after the publication of *Ulysses*, he asked her, 'Send me any news you like, programmes, pawntickets, press cuttings, handbills. I like reading them' (*LI* 194).

For all Joyce's concern with the naturalistic details of external reality, in essential respects the true epic of *Ulysses* is an internal one – both physically and mentally. He claimed to Jan Parandowski that 'for too long were the stars studied and man's insides neglected. An eclipse of the sun could be predicted many centuries before anyone knew which way the blood circulated in our bodies' (*PAE* 159). But above all his revolution was in the presentation of the psyche: 'the modern theme', he told Arthur Power, 'is the subterranean forces, those hidden tides which govern everything and run humanity counter to the apparent flood' (Power 54). The imagery of 'tides' and 'flood' suggests a term that Joyce himself never used: 'stream of consciousness'.

In William James's *The Principles of Psychology* (1890) we read that consciousness 'does not appear to itself chopped up in bits', so words like 'chain' or 'train' are inappropriate: 'It is nothing jointed; it flows. A "river" or a "stream" are the metaphors by which it is most naturally described. *In talking of it hereafter, let us call it the stream of thought, of consciousness, or of subjective life*' (James, I 239). In its literary sense, the term is not easy to define precisely, but it has come to refer to the current of associations going on uninterruptedly in our minds: the flux of thoughts, sensations, and feelings that we all experience, the direction of which is determined by associative rather than 'logical' channels. Stream of consciousness fiction, then, records or depicts that flow in various ways and at various levels, all the way from the unconscious itself through the preconscious to the conscious, to use Freud's terms. Such fiction has been profoundly important in the twentieth century, although it had numerous pre-cursors: one thinks of Sterne, Poe, Melville, Henry James, Tolstoy, and even of poets like Browning and Shakespeare.

But the person James Joyce always credited with having revealed to him the possibilities of this method was a then almost unknown French novelist, Édouard Dujardin, the author of *Les lauriers sont coupés* (1887), eventually translated as *We'll to the Woods No More*, which Joyce had bought at a railway station in Paris in 1903 (*JJ* 126). In later years Joyce described his method as one in which 'I try to give the unspoken, unacted thoughts of people in the way they occur. But I'm not the first one to do it. I took it from Dujardin. You don't know Dujardin? You should' (Budgen, *Making* 92). His insist-ence on his debt to Dujardin was often greeted with incredulity, but there is evidence that backs his claim – such as a letter of 1917 to Dujardin asking him where he might find a copy of *Les lauriers sont coupés*, his own being unavailable to him, and describing himself as a sincere admirer of Dujardin's work (*LII* 409). Later he signed Dujardin's copy of *Ulysses* as 'le larron impénitent' – the impenitent thief (*LI* 287). He would even take time off from the work on *Finnegans Wake* to help Stuart Gilbert in the translation of Dujardin's novel, which has evidence of Joyce's hand.

Dujardin's novel is a short book, in which we are restricted to the thoughts or stream of consciousness of the protagonist, Daniel Prince; the result is inventive and original, and extremely interesting from a literary historical perspective. Still, the novel's limitations and the awkwardness resulting from its slavish adherence to its innovative method bring out all the more forcefully what Joyce was to do with the basic approach and his important modifications of it. The fame of *Ulysses* eventually brought a measure of fame to Dujardin, who then wrote a book in which he discussed the techniques he had used: *Le Monologue intérieur, son apparition, ses origines, sa place dans l'œuvre de James Joyce* (1931). '*Monologue intérieur*', or 'interior monologue', has become a term as ubiquitous as stream of consciousness. Dujardin, who did not originate the term, described the interior monologue as consisting of words or speech ('*discours*') without a listener and in fact unspoken, in which a character's deepest thoughts, those nearest the unconscious, are presented totally without logical organisation, in a mode which gives the impression that the original thoughts are actually being reproduced (*Monologue* 59). In the simplest terms, the interior monologue may be regarded as a device or a technique, while the stream of consciousness is what it often records.

Of course, for all his protestations, others had influenced Joyce as well; perhaps the most fascinating possibility is Stanislaus, who in 1924 pointed out in a letter that he had practised in his diary, which his brother used to read, the recording of 'rambling thoughts – and of a person lying awake in bed, too' (*LIII* 106); Stannie was specifically thinking of an entry dated 18 July 1904, which begins 'I'm an unlucky, bloody, bloody, bloody fool. Och! I can't curse big enough! I wanted to go to this Regatta with Katsy tomorrow, I wanted to go! Curse on this ankle of mine!' As he portrays himself getting drowsier, the entry concludes: 'M – said that – . What was his name? – I just caught the name, just! – Who's this said that? – Who's this? – I can't – What's this the thing was? – I can't think – remember – Dawn! – A – ah! – sink! – "A – a – a – ah multitude" – multitude – ude — . And so, sleep' (*Diary* 165, 167). The full entry does indeed make fascinating reading as a possible germ of the process that his brother so perfected.

If Joyce found sources for his techniques in his reading, he found sources for his characters in the world around him – and in himself. Clearly Stephen Dedalus is an autobiographical figure, although in fact Joyce's attitude towards him was becoming even more distant in some respects than it was in his treatment of Stephen in the *Portrait*; as he remarked to Budgen, 'I haven't let this young man off very lightly, have I? Many writers have written about themselves. I wonder if any of them has been as candid as I have?' (*Making* 51). Another exchange with Budgen suggests his own

growing identification not so much with Stephen as with Leopold
Bloom: 'I have just got a letter asking me why I don't give Bloom a
rest', he reported while the novel was appearing serially in the *Little
Review*; 'The writer of it wants more Stephen. But Stephen no longer
interests me to the same extent.'⁵ When he made that remark in 1919,
Joyce was thirty-seven, a year younger than Bloom and fifteen years
older than Stephen.

But other people as well as Joyce himself contributed to the characterisation of Bloom. The original idea for a short story called
'*Ulysses*' centred on a Mr Hunter he had known in Dublin (*LII* 168);
his full name was Alfred H. Hunter, and Joyce apparently believed
– erroneously, as it turns out – that he was Jewish. We do not know
much at all about him: in *The Jews of Ireland* Louis Hyman reports
that Hunter resided in Clonliffe Road, was the son of a shoemaker,
and in 1898 had married Margaret Cummins, who had lived in
Rathmines very near where Joyce lived between the ages of two and
five; Hunter had an office on Clare Street which was next to that of
two dentists, both named Bloom (and one of whom is mentioned in
Ulysses); his name appears in the *Freeman's Journal* of 14 July 1904
among the mourners at the funeral for Matthew Kane, a friend of
Joyce's father and one of the models for the fictional Martin
Cunningham (Hyman 169). Ellmann says that it was rumoured that
Hunter had an unfaithful wife; Hyman cannot corroborate that but
tells of a Joseph Blum (later Bloom) whose wife, when he emigrated,
was said to have become mistress to another man.⁶

It is possible that Hunter came to Joyce's rescue (much as Bloom
does for Stephen in the Circe chapter of *Ulysses*) in June 1904
after Joyce had been knocked down in St Stephen's Green; Joyce
received, according to Gogarty's account, 'a black eye – the "gift of
an angry lover" whose lady he had importuned being ignorant of
her lover's presence' (*Many Lives* 12). Cosgrave was present at that
incident but instead of helping his friend stood aside with his hands
in his pockets (*Workshop* 93). Ellmann reports a rumour that Hunter
helped Joyce get up and took him home, but the evidence seems
inconclusive.⁷

In any case, Hunter and Joyce himself shared Bloom with other
models as well, to varying degrees. We have already noticed the
physical characteristics Bloom shares with Byrne, and how much
Svevo's Jewishness went into the characterisation, as did other aspects of his background, such as, specifically, the fact that Svevo's
father, like Bloom's, was a poor Jew from Hungary (Furbank 90).

Richard Ellmann also cites an advertising canvasser in Dublin named Charles Chance, who had served as a model for C. P. M'Coy in the story 'Grace', and Teodoro Mayer, the Hungarian-Jewish publisher of *Il Piccolo della Sera* (*JJ* 196, 374–5). Leopold Bloom needed many models if he was to be a worthy counterpart to the 'complete all-round character' of Ulysses; for Bloom too was to be, Joyce told Budgen, 'a complete man as well' – and, he added, 'a good man. At any rate, that is what I intend that he shall be.' At another time he told his friend, 'As the day wears on Bloom should overshadow them all' (Budgen, *Making* 17, 116).

Readers of *Ulysses* have noticed the Blooms' unusual practice of sleeping head-to-foot to each other; at least for a time during their life in Trieste, the Joyces did the same (*LII* 202). There are of course much more essential ways in which the fictional marriage comes out of the author's – and Molly out of Nora (who, however, always responded to such a suggestion by saying no, 'She was much fatter' [*N* 265]).

Joyce's original idea for the Penelope chapter was to write it in the form of a number of Molly Bloom's letters, in prose patterned after Nora's. In a sweeping generalisation, in a letter to Stannie in 1906, and after interpolating within his letter a totally unpunctuated one from Nora, Joyce asked, 'Do you notice how women when they write disregard stops and capital letters?' (*LII* 173).

Recent feminist criticism has debated the existence and nature of what the French critic Hélène Cixous has called *écriture féminine*, or female writing.[8] (Cixous and others stress that *écriture féminine* may be written by men as well as women: it is the writing which is gendered, so to speak, regardless of the gender of the author.) A great deal of the debate has centred on whether 'female writing' exists at all – and, if it does, on whether it is an expression of the physical body and the unconscious: fluid, subversive and unrepressed, not predetermined and restricted by male patriarchal reason, codes and categories. Part of the controversy has entailed whether such a concept reinforces crude and distorting stereotypes of women as instinctive, non-rational, 'primitive', and so on. In the context of a discussion of *Ulysses* the concept of *écriture féminine* brings up aspects of stream of consciousness fiction we have already looked at, and the specific interior monologues of the non-stereotypical males Stephen Dedalus and Leopold Bloom – the latter explicitly called 'the new womanly man' (*Ulysses* 403 [15.1798–9]). But obviously it is, above all, suggestive in terms of Molly's monologue at the end of the novel, in pages which 'disregard' most rules of punctuation. In her essay 'The Laugh of the Medusa' Cixous, who has written a biography of Joyce, cites Molly Bloom as 'carrying *Ulysses* off beyond any book and toward the new writing' (255).

One of the intriguing things in regard to Joyce's odd generalisation – his perception that women's writing lacked punctuation – is that it is borne out by the letters we have from several of the women in his life to whom he was closest, none of whom had received extensive formal education: his mother, his Aunt Josephine, and above all his wife. For example, here is the final paragraph from a 1912 letter from Nora while she was in Galway:

> well Jim I hope you are minding yourself and how is poor little Georgie I hope he is well dear be sure and dont let him eat too much tell him I will send him something for his birthday my uncle as after taking his holidays he had to get a bone cut out of his nose Mother says he spent a buckett full of money so that I am afraid its not possible for you to come on at any rate I will let you know if I have any further news remember me to Stannie Good-bye love and keep well [*LII* 297]

In another letter during that stay she started out with more periods – six in the first eleven lines – but as she warmed up she neglected them entirely, and there is not another one in the thirty-two remaining lines of the letter.[9] Molly's monologue may or may not be usefully seen as an example of *écriture féminine*, but in any case it does seem an imitation, with a vengeance, of Nora's writing.

* * *

In Tom Stoppard's play *Travesties*, which is in large part about Joyce's existence in Zurich while writing *Ulysses*, a character quite unsympathetic to the novelist remembers having demanded of him what he would be able to say years later when asked, 'And what did you do in the Great War?'; he also recalls the infuriating reply: 'I wrote *Ulysses*. . . . What did you do?'[10]

Not surprisingly, the war years were ones of major disruption and instability for the Joyces, who in a five-year period lived in three different countries. They left Trieste for Zurich in 1915, returned to Trieste in 1919, and then left again – this time for Paris – the year after that. They had come to Zurich because of the war; when it broke out in August 1914, Trieste – as part of the Austro-Hungarian Empire but with a largely Italian population – was a tense city. All Irredentists (those who wished Trieste, for example, to become Italian) were suspect, including Stanislaus, whose lack of discretion in voicing his sympathies led him to be interned in Austria from January 1915 until the end of the war. Nevertheless Joyce and his family tried to stay on, as he continued to work on his new novel. But with the entry of Italy into the war on the side of the Allies in May 1915, it became necessary for them, as British citizens, to leave. The logical destination seemed neutral Switzerland; they left Trieste by train 28 June and arrived in Zurich two days later, where they stopped – so Joyce wrote Harriet Shaw Weaver – merely because it was 'the first big city after the frontier'. He still did not know if it would be where they would settle (*LI* 82). They were in a difficult situation and with little or no money; Nora's uncle Michael Healy immediately and very generously sent them fifteen pounds (a much larger sum at the time than it sounds today) and continued to help by sending them funds until the end of the war. Additional help came from Ireland through the efforts of Yeats, who arranged for Joyce to receive a grant of seventy-five pounds from the Royal Literary Fund (*JJ* 390, 392). So the Joyces remained, in a city with great political and cultural ferment: it was from Zurich that Lenin left in 1917 on a train bound for Russia, and it was from that city too that Tristan Tzara and others were sending Dada into the world.

The world of Ireland was also undergoing a revolution. The Easter Rising took place in 1916, and during the ensuing battles Francis Sheehy-Skeffington was summarily executed by a mad British officer. Joyce was of course not alone in being moved with complex emotions by the events occurring in his native land, and one day when Budgen speculated that many Irish people would not much like *Ulysses*, Joyce replied that he realised that that was inevitable but worried that the book might appear to be 'the work of a cynic. I don't want to hurt or offend those of my countrymen who are devoting their lives to a cause they feel to be necessary and just' (*Making* 152).

His intense belief in the cause of an independent Ireland produced great sympathy for those rebelling against the British; but his perhaps even greater abhorrence of violence produced mixed feelings which became especially complex when the controversies over the treaty which divided the island and brought about the creation of the Irish Free State led to a fierce civil war in 1922. Ironically, it was at that time that Nora decided to return to Ireland, against Joyce's strong objections, and she took the children as well. While they were in Galway, fighting broke out between the opposing forces; Irish Republican Army troops seized a warehouse across from where they were staying, causing Irish Free State troops to use their windows to fire back with machine guns; frightened, Nora and the children left the city – only to have their train fired upon by both sides during their journey, causing them to have to lie on their stomachs. Joyce was understandably disturbed and angry upon hearing what had happened, but in his readiness to perceive conspiracies against his own person – in what others might even call his paranoia – he mysteriously yet vehemently regarded these attacks as aimed at him and as evidence of 'malignancy and treachery' (*LI* 189–90, 311).

In Zurich during the war Joyce supplemented the money he was receiving from other sources with teaching private pupils. Pressures were great, and late in 1916 he even reported to Harriet Shaw Weaver that he had suffered several collapses which his doctor attributed to a nervous breakdown (*LI* 97). Nevertheless he made good progress on *Ulysses* and during his leisure time became involved in a troupe organised to put on plays. The idea was that of an actor, Claud W. Sykes, with whom he had become friends; in 1918 Joyce became the business manager of what they called the English Players (*JJ* 423). Their first production was Oscar Wilde's *The Importance of Being Earnest*, and they chose as the actor for the part of Algernon a young man named Henry Carr, who worked at the British Consulate (it was Carr who became the basis for the central figure of Stoppard's *Travesties*).

Carr and the others did a good job, but afterwards there was a dispute over how much Carr should be paid and, especially, over whether he should receive a reimbursement for the expense of the clothes he had purchased for his role. Joyce became annoyed and in his anger confronted Carr at the consulate and demanded money from the sales of tickets which Carr had been given. Joyce later claimed that he left after Carr used abusive language; in a letter to the British Minister at Berne, Sir Horace Rumbold, he asserted that Carr 'threatened to "wring my neck the next time he met me in the street". I replied "That is not language that should be used in a government office" and thereupon left the office' (*LII* 425). (Joyce also wrote, he reported to Budgen, to the British Prime Minister, David Lloyd George: 'I always appeal to the highest instance', he told his friend, just as 'Stephen appeals from Father Dolan to Father Conmee' [*Making* 197].)

For a while, his fight seemed successful. In their complicated countersuits against one another, Joyce won in his claim for the money for the tickets for which Carr had been responsible (*JJ* 445). Meanwhile the English Players had gone on to produce an evening of short plays, one of which was Synge's *Riders to the Sea*, in which Nora played Cathleen, and Giorgio and Lucia had small parts, while Joyce himself sang from offstage (*N* 211), as he did again during a production of Browning's *In a Balcony*; less happy was the result of follow-up legal proceedings in which Joyce was ordered early in 1919 to pay both damages and court costs (*JJ* 447, 452). He obtained his revenge against the representatives of the British establishment by putting their names into *Ulysses*: Rumbold became the '*Master Barber*' who applies for a position as hangman in the Cyclops chapter, and Carr the loutish British soldier who knocks Stephen down in Circe (249 [12.431]; 491 [4747–8]).

Joyce's friend Mary Colum has observed that while he seems to have had 'what might be called a persecution complex', that is 'not really surprising, for he actually was persecuted' (127). At least he was as an artist, for he continued to face immense problems of censorship. Once again his point man in the struggle for his work was Pound, who sent the first three chapters of *Ulysses* to Margaret Anderson and Jane Heap, the editors of an American avant-garde magazine, the *Little Review*; in her memoir, Anderson recalls her reaction when she came upon the opening of Proteus ('Ineluctable modality of the visible . . .'):

> This is the most beautiful thing we'll ever have, I cried. We'll print it if it's the last effort of our lives.
>
> James Joyce's "Ulysses" began in the *Little Review* in March, 1918. We ran it month after month for three years and four times the issues containing it were burned by order of the United States Post Office, because of alleged obscenity.
>
> [*My Thirty Years' War* 174–5]

Matters came to a head with the fourth confiscation and burning, of the July–August 1920 issue, which contained a portion of Nausicaa, one problem being – according to the *New York Times* – 'too frank expression concerning woman's dress when the woman was in the clothes described' (quoted in Fitch 76).

It is perhaps difficult fully to comprehend the problems Anderson and Heap faced as publishers without a historical understanding of the daring nature of much of what Joyce was doing. Even Ezra Pound argued with Joyce that he had gone too far: 'you use a stronger word than you need, and this is bad art. . . . The excrements will prevent people from noticing the quality of things contrasted.' Pound himself censored portions of *Ulysses* before sending it on to be printed in the *Little Review*, deleting from the Calypso chapter, for example, references to Bloom's 'bowels', to his 'undoing the waist-band of his trousers', and to how 'he allowed his bowels to ease themselves quietly as he read' and 'tore away half the prize story sharply and wiped himself with it' (Pound 131, 301–2). John Quinn, the prominent lawyer who defended Anderson and Heap in court, also privately objected to much of the book's language, although like Pound he believed that some passages which were objectionable for a magazine to be sent through the mails would be suitable in a book (Reid 443).

Anderson and Heap were brought to trial in February 1921; when the Assistant District Attorney proposed to read some of the offend-ing passages aloud, one of the judges objected, pointing to the pres-ence of a young woman in the courtroom – Margaret Anderson. Quinn countered that after all she was one of the publishers, but the judge replied that he was 'sure she didn't know the significance of what she was publishing' (Anderson 221). Anderson and Heap lost the case, had to pay a fine, and could no longer continue to serialise *Ulysses*.

There are several ironies in the difficulties *Ulysses* had with cen-sorship and in the shock it gave to many sensitive and intelligent readers – like Stanislaus, who when it was published concluded that 'everything dirty' seemed to have the same irresistible attraction for his brother 'that cow-dung has for flies' (*LIII* 58). After all, anyone picking up a copy of *Ulysses* for pornographic thrills was – and is – likely to come away from it feeling distinctly disappointed. And, too, the controversial passages came from a man who – despite the erotic power of the explicit letters he had written to his wife in 1909 – was by his own account and according to all his friends notably reserved if not prudish in his conversation. Mary Colum says she 'never heard him make a remark that would embarrass a nun' (140); Arthur Power records that 'in the Joyces' home there were never any dirty stories told; even risky ones were taboo, and if anyone started telling

them they did not last long as a friend' (71); and having been rep-
rimanded by Joyce for telling a joke that produced the reaction, 'I
never say that kind of thing ... though I write it', Italo Svevo was led
to reflect that 'it seems that his own books cannot be read in his
presence' (*James Joyce* n.p. [25]).

Thus the author of some of the most revolutionary works of his
time could seem, in some respects, quite traditional; the creator of
some of the most complex art of the twentieth century was, he often
said at any rate, in many ways a very 'simple' person: he claimed to
Budgen, 'if there is any difficulty in reading what I write it is because
of the material I use. In my case the thought is always simple.'[11] The
man who had begun his adulthood by asserting in 'The Day of the
Rabblement' that 'no man ... can be a lover of the true or the good
unless he abhors the multitude' (*CW* 69) came round to professing
that 'nobody seems to be inclined to present me to the world in my
unadorned prosaicness' (*LI* 178) and frequently spoke of his bourgeois life and personality, indeed even art: he told Power, 'I suppose
my work is middleclass' (110) – precisely what Wyndham Lewis
accused it of being in *Time and Western Man* (77).

It is valuable to recognise how much James Joyce was in touch
with ordinary people and everyday life, and how in many respects
he shared the values of the world around him – but not in all ways.
For it is not merely that, as Stephen claims of Shakespeare, 'he passes
on towards eternity in undiminished personality, untaught by the
wisdom he has written or by the laws he has revealed' (*U* 162
[9.476–7]): despite the increasing importance in Joyce's world of a
veneer of conventionality, his was undeniably an unusual life, and
certainly his thought could be as complex and as radical as his art.

Even before the publication of *Ulysses* as a book, that art was
attracting attention in other ways besides censorship. In 1918 he
received notice from a bank that an anonymous benefactor had
donated 12 000 francs which he would receive over a period of
twelve months. Very soon Joyce managed to find out that the donor
was Mrs Harold McCormick; she was also a patron of Carl Gustav
Jung, who, like Mrs McCormick, lived in Zurich (*JJ* 422). The latter
interest led to a break with Joyce and an end to her patronage, when
he refused to agree to her suggestion that he be analysed by – as
Joyce put it in a letter to Harriet Shaw Weaver – 'a certain Doctor
Jung (the Swiss Tweedledum who is not to be confused with the
Viennese Tweedledee, Dr Freud)' (*LI* 166).

Weaver herself was a much more reliable and sympathetic source of aid, monetary and otherwise. Before Mrs McCormick's gift there had been another anonymous one, in 1917, of £200; it was from Weaver, who two years later, again anonymously, added a much larger gift of £5000, to be held in trust with the capital not to be touched (*DMW* 134–5, 157). Joyce naturally sought to discover the identity of his patron and was on the wrong scent (he thought it was Lady Cunard) when in July 1919, to forestall awkwardness, Weaver wrote to him revealing her identity as the person who had made the gifts. In his reply, he spoke to her of his feelings during the two years in which he had received her generous gifts as ones of 'foreboding', as he feared that each episode of *Ulysses* as it appeared would 'alienate gradually the sympathy of the person who was helping me'; he now saw that such fears were groundless, and as a token of his gratitude he asked her to accept the manuscript of the *Portrait* (*SL* 240–1).

They had still not met and did not do so until after the publication of *Ulysses* as a book in 1922, when Joyce made a trip to London in August of that year; they were both very favourably impressed by the meeting; she noticed but decided not to be excessively disturbed by his extravagance with the money she had given him (*DMW* 201–2), and there would be additional gifts in later years. She also hoped to publish an English edition of *Ulysses*, as she had of the *Portrait*, and she bought up the rights to all his books that had thus far been published by other firms: *Chamber Music*, *Dubliners*, and *Exiles* (*DMW* 189). Aside from her activities for Joyce she did not publish a great deal, but what she did was notable: for example the first editions of T. S. Eliot's *Prufrock and Other Observations* and Marianne Moore's *Poems*.

By all accounts Harriet Shaw Weaver was an extraordinary person: 'Saint Harriet', Lucia Joyce called her (a 'patron saint' Rebecca West specified).[12] To Joyce she was more than merely a source of income, and while it may or may not be true that she was another 'mother-figure' upon whom he depended, as has been claimed,[13] it became increasingly important to him that he continue to receive her intellectual and spiritual support; in 1925, sending her a section of what was to become *Finnegans Wake*, he wrote, 'I shall be anxious to hear what you think of it', and 'I hope you will write to me about it' (*SL* 305). They were both quite formal in social relationships; neither, for example, liked to be addressed by their first names: except to family members, he would be 'Joyce' or 'Mr Joyce', she always 'Miss

Weaver'. But for all their formality with each other, they were friends, and she remained an unfailingly loyal one.

There were other friends as well during the Zurich years, of course, such as Ottocaro Weiss, from Trieste, and Paul Ruggiero, who worked for a Swiss bank. Above all there was the Englishman Frank Budgen, who had been a seaman and was now a painter, although supporting himself with other work, including occasional modelling for other artists (he was, for example, the model for the sailor on the pack of Player's cigarettes [*N* 214]). The two men became extremely close, and on walks through the city or in pubs and cafés Joyce inundated his receptive and intelligent friend with ideas about and for his novel; as Budgen put it, 'he was in respect of *Ulysses* naturally the Ancient Mariner and I the Wedding Guest' (*Myselves* 184).

As the novel progressed the task of explaining and even defending his procedures to at least some of his friends seemed to become necessary. We have seen Pound's reservations about the importance of Bloom and some of the frank language; he also wondered whether the technique of the Sirens chapter went too far (*LI* 128); Joyce also worried that Weaver might 'begin to regard the various styles of the episodes with dismay and prefer the initial style' (*LI* 129). Much has been made of Joyce's remark, once, that he had put 'so many enigmas and puzzles' into *Ulysses* 'that it will keep the professors busy for centuries arguing over what I meant, and that's the only way of insuring one's immortality' (*JJ* 521). But he also passionately argued that his method was artistically essential; he wrote to Weaver that, for example, the variation in the chapter styles, 'I beg you to believe, is not capricious' (*LI* 129). Some early critics of the novel regarded it as a huge hoax, but no careful reader would be likely to call it 'capricious' or careless; Joyce worked on it with astounding intensity. He claimed that the Oxen of the Sun chapter 'cost me about 1000 hours' work' (*LI* 141), and one could imagine that to be an underestimate. Circe, he acknowledged, 'presents for me great technical difficulties and for the reader something worse' (*LI* 143).

While he was working on the Penelope episode in 1921 he informed Weaver that he had finished its first sentence, 'but as this contains about 2500 words the deed is more than it seems to be' (*LI* 168). He was working on the Ithaca chapter around the same time and actually finished it last. He described it to Claud Sykes as 'a mathematico-astronomico-physico-mechanico-geometrico-chemico sublimation of Bloom and Stephen (devil take 'em both) to prepare for the final amplitudinously curvilinear episode of Penelope' (*LI* 164). As what he called 'the ugly duckling of the book', Ithaca was his favourite chapter of all (Budgen, *Making* 258).

Joyce's work on the novel was made even more difficult by the fact that he had to find typists in a country – by then he was in Paris – where English was of course not the native language; in the case of one typist, her husband proved to be still another self-appointed censor of Joyce's art. A Mrs Harrison was typing the manuscript of Circe in April 1921 when her husband, who worked at the British Embassy, came across it and then proceeded to tear up and burn what he had read; the agitated Mrs Harrison managed to protect and hide most of the manuscript, however, and returned it to Joyce within a couple of days, only a few pages having been destroyed (*LIII* 40; *LI* 161).

Another acute source of stress, which would remain serious in varying degrees for the rest of his life, was eye trouble. In August 1917 he was walking in the street when he suffered an attack of glaucoma so severe that he was 'incapacitated' and unable to move for about twenty minutes (*SL* 226). Within a week he had surgery performed on his right eye: he would have to undergo ten more operations over the course of a decade and a half, and in 1923 he also had to have all his teeth removed because of related infection.[14] Attacks so severe they left him 'rolling over the carpet' in pain (*LI* 168) abated by the mid-1930s, but he would never really be relieved of his severe eye problems.

Some of Joyce's problems were of his own creation. For example one way in which he attempted to alleviate the varying pressures and sources of stress was, apparently, to engage in affairs – or, perhaps, mere flirtations: we cannot be sure. On a holiday in Locarno recommended by his eye doctor in 1917, he seems to have become attracted to Gertrude Kaempffer, a young doctor recovering from tuberculosis. According to accounts Dr Kaempffer wrote over forty-five years later, Joyce tried to begin an affair or at least a correspondence, both in Locarno and afterward when they met by chance in Zurich, but she was hesitant and nothing came of it (*JJ* 418–19).

It is not clear precisely how much more success Joyce had with Martha (or Marthe) Fleischmann, a young woman he walked by as she was entering her front door; her later recollection to Heinrich Straumann was that Joyce stopped with an expression of 'wonder' in his face and then apologised, explaining that she 'reminded him of a girl he once had seen standing on the beach in his home country' –

the original, of course, for the wading girl of the *Portrait*.[15] Joyce began a correspondence with Fleischmann, who was the mistress of an engineer, Rudolf Hiltpold; in one of his letters Joyce expressed the hunch – and apparently the desire – that she was Jewish, but she was not. Like Bloom in his letters to *his* Martha in *Ulysses*, Joyce used 'Greek ees' instead of Roman ones in signing his name.[16]

Joyce put Budgen in the uncomfortable position of helping him in his affair; Budgen was of course reluctant – in addition to all the other reasons he would naturally have for not wanting to get involved with what Joyce was doing, he greatly admired Nora – but yielded when Joyce told him, 'if I permitted myself to be under any restraint in this matter it would be spiritual death to me', a statement which Budgen interpreted as meaning that he would 'be guilty of stultifying his art'. In any case Budgen's role was small; he hesitantly agreed to host both Fleischmann and Joyce on the latter's birthday in 1919. Joyce prepared for the visit by inspecting Budgen's flat, which he found suitable except that Budgen's paintings seemed 'too chaste'; Budgen offered to do some charcoal nudes within the next hour, while Joyce – still connecting Fleischmann with Jewishness – went off to borrow a menorah. When the couple arrived later, Budgen was not particularly impressed; they did not stay long, and when Budgen met Joyce some hours later 'he told me in an aside that he had explored that evening the coldest and hottest parts of a woman's body' (*Myselves* 190–4). Despite that comment, the evidence is inconclusive, and it is possible that Joyce and Fleischmann did not actually consummate their affair. Joyce wrote to Budgen in June that he had not seen her since the afternoon in his friend's flat in February – but that Hiltpold had written him 'a threatening violent letter' after having found out about him when Fleischmann had a breakdown; Joyce surrendered all of her letters to him (*SL* 239).

Joyce did not waste experience: part of his relationship with Martha Fleischmann went into the creation of Bloom's correspondence with Martha Clifford, but it also contributed to Bloom's interest in Gerty MacDowell – Martha was lame, like Gerty (Budgen, *Myselves* 194) – although, for that matter, it was Gertrude Kaempffer's first name that Joyce gave to Gerty.

Bloom becomes on Bloomsday a 'cuckold', and if Joyce dallied with other women, he seemed in part of his being to wish Nora to flirt with other men – again for the sake of his art, he believed: according to Budgen again, Nora tearfully told him one night 'that Jim wanted her to "go with other men so that he would have something to write about'".[17] This bizarre request is even more astonishing than it would ordinarily be when we recall the frenzy of Joyce's distraught reaction to Cosgrave's accusations about a decade earlier. There is no sign that Nora yielded to Joyce in his strange wish: Nora was a fiercely independent woman, resisting even requests that clearly meant a good deal more to her husband than that one – like his plea in April 1922, months after the publication of *Ulysses*, that she 'even now . . . read that terrible book which has now broken the heart in my breast' (*LIII* 63).

It is possible but by no means certain that both Joyce's own flirtations and his suggestions that Nora might 'go with other men' arose out of their having ceased to have complete sex with one another by around 1917[18] – perhaps as Leopold and Molly Bloom have ceased engaging in 'complete carnal intercourse, with ejaculation of semen within the natural female organ' (*U* 605 [17.2278–9]).

While it is possible nevertheless to say of perhaps both Joyce and Bloom what Sylvia Beach said of Joyce, that 'his marriage . . . was one of the best pieces of luck that ever befell him' (42), there were still other points of friction between Joyce and Nora. Notably, there was her concern about his drinking; in response, he restricted himself to wine (he rarely drank hard liquor in any case); his preference was for white wine, especially the Swiss Fendant de Sion (*JJ* 455). But he could get drunk on wine, after all, and besides Nora another person to be very disturbed at the stories she heard of his drinking was Harriet Shaw Weaver, to whom alcohol was 'a great evil' (*DMW* 184); for his part Joyce was troubled by her reaction to what she had heard and hastened to reassure her – in a doggedly ironic letter – that 'a nice collection could be made of legends about me', such as the one that gave him 'the reputation of being an incurable dipsomaniac' (*SL* 282). Although he was very careful never under any circumstances to drink during the daytime,[19] it is probably true that he did drink more than he should have, and certainly he did so on nights when he would have to be helped home. In Trieste, at least, there had been the pressures toward moderation exerted by Stanislaus, but they were not present in Zurich. That was to change: for the Joyces decided to return to Trieste at the end of the war.

The armistice was declared in November 1918, but the Joyces did not leave Zurich until almost a year later, in October 1919. In the meantime, Stanislaus had been released from his internment in Austria. The Joyces had been nostalgic about Trieste, and in Zurich as well as, later, in Paris, they continued to speak Italian within the family. But Trieste, which was now part of Italy and in economic decline, was not the same – and not merely because, as Joyce wrote to Pound, he disliked 'returning to places'. In the same letter he spoke of their crowded conditions: they lived 'in a flat with eleven other people' (actually ten others).[20] Inflation had also hit Trieste very hard, and they had a difficult time financially. Joyce resisted giving lessons again, although he did resume his teaching at the Scuola Superiore, which was now becoming a university; his commitment was only six hours a week, but he planned to resign 'as it wastes my time and my nerves' (*LII* 468).

For six weeks he was unable to get back to *Ulysses*, but he finally started the Nausicaa chapter and found the going slow (*LI* 134). He greatly missed his Zurich friends; after seven months he claimed to Pound that 'since I came here I suppose I have not exchanged 100 words with anybody' (*LII* 468). Above all he missed the long conversations with Budgen about the progress of his novel, and in a series of letters he urged – begged – his friend to join him in Trieste. Budgen, although he too missed their times together, resisted. Meanwhile Joyce made up for their lack of talk with detailed descriptions in his correspondence of what he was doing in his book – for example he wrote that '*Nausikaa* is written in a namby-pamby jammy marmalady drawersy (alto là!) style with effects of incense, mariolatry, masturbation, stewed cockles, painter's palette, chit chat, circumlocution, etc., etc.' (*LI* 135).

In earlier times the role of whetstone would have been played by Stanislaus, but, Joyce lamented to Budgen, his brother thought *Ulysses* a mere 'joke', had after all been four years in internment, and 'has a devil of a lot to do and likes a gay elegant life in his own set' (*LI* 134). During Stanislaus's internment, the Joyces had done what they could for him, and Nora especially sent him as many packages of food and other items as she could (*N* 189). Yet back in Trieste some of the old resentments returned, and the two brothers were never again as intimate as they once had been. After Joyce moved to Paris and *Ulysses* had been published, Stanislaus wrote him, with no attempt to conceal his bitterness, of 'the careless indifference with which you have always acted in affairs that concerned me. I am no longer a boy' (*LIII* 59). Moreover, Stanislaus came to feel less and less sympathy with his brother's work; yet they continued to correspond, although less frequently than before, and were able to get together several times before Joyce's death. On one of those occasions Joyce met Stannie's new wife Nelly, whom he had married in August 1928. Still later, in 1936, when the Italian fascists ordered Stanislaus to leave Italy, Joyce was able to use his influence to postpone the edict indefinitely, although for a time Stanislaus was deprived of his employment – the position at the university which had been his brother's (*JJ* 603, 689, 697).

Joyce's loneliness in Trieste was one of the factors that made him so eager to get together with a friend and supporter he had yet to meet – Ezra Pound. He tried to get Pound to visit Trieste, but finally in June 1920, when Pound was staying at Sirmione (near Verona on Lake Garda), Joyce decided that he would visit him, overcoming his intense fear of thunder. He had heard there were storms in the area; but, as he wrote to Harriet Shaw Weaver with bizarre irony, 'in spite of my dread of thunderstorms and detestation of travelling I went there bringing my son with me to act as a lightning conductor' (*LI* 142). Pound urged him to leave Trieste and come to Paris to see about the publication of his books. Certainly the situation in Trieste – economically, politically (with the early rise of the fascists) and, for Joyce, psychologically and personally – had become untenable; so he determined to leave Italy, although at first he intended only to stop off in Paris 'for a week or so' on the way to settling in London (*LII* 472). The Joyces arrived 8 July 1920 and stayed there after all – remaining until forced into still another exile by World War II, twenty years later.

The Paris of the 1920s has become the stuff of myth even more than of history, but at the time too it seemed that, in the words of Joyce's friend Nino Frank, 'in those days every intellectual in the world lived for Paris' (*PAE* 75). It attracted artists from around the globe. Mentioning only a few of just the expatriate writers whose careers in the city became famous – Gertrude Stein, Ernest Hemingway, Djuna Barnes, F. Scott Fitzgerald, Henry Miller, Vladimir Nabokov, H. D. – calls up a world of legend and cultural excitement unsurpassed in the twentieth century; in time, the most legendary figure of them all was James Joyce.

Not the least of the reasons for the popularity of Paris with artists was that it was relatively inexpensive; but Joyce was not one to find it easy to economise anywhere. He needed money and thought of taking up teaching again (*JJ* 489), but one of Harriet Shaw Weaver's gifts enabled him to devote his time to *Ulysses*. By the summer of 1921 he was able to tell the French critic, novelist and translator Valery Larbaud the answer to a question his new friend had once asked – what the last word of the novel would be: 'La voilà: yes'. But in fact the last chapter to be finished was Ithaca, at the end of October 1921 (*LI* 169, 175).

Joyce had worked on *Ulysses* for seven years, but it was one thing to write it, another to find a publisher willing or able to publish it. Weaver would have liked to have done so in England, but by then she had exhausted all possibilities with English printers. One of her early attempts, at the suggestion of T. S. Eliot, whose *Prufrock and Other Observations* she had published, was to approach the people who were about to publish his *Poems*: Leonard and Virginia Woolf, who ran the small Hogarth Press. Weaver visited them in 1918 to discuss the matter, carrying with her the portions of the novel that Joyce had thus far completed. Leonard Woolf would later recall her as 'a very mild blueeyed advanced spinster'; Virginia Woolf's record in her diary, while more detailed, also stresses Weaver's appearance, which Woolf found incongruous with what she expected the editor of the daring *Egoist* to look like:

> I did my best to make her reveal herself, in spite of her appear-ance, all that the Editress of the Egoist ought to be, but she re-mained inalterably modest judicious & decorous. Her neat mauve suit fitted both soul & body; her grey gloves laid straight by her plate symbolised domestic rectitude; her table manners were those of a well bred hen. We could get no talk to go. Possibly the poor woman was impeded by her sense that what she had in the brownpaper parcel was quite out of keeping with her own con-tents. But then how did she ever come in contact with Joyce & the rest? Why does their filth seek exit from her mouth? Heaven knows. She is incompetent from the business point of view & was uncertain what arrangements to make. We both looked at the MS. which seems to be an attempt to push the bounds of expression further on, but still all in the same direction.[21]

Yet the Woolfs were impressed enough to decide that they would publish the novel if they could find a printer who would handle it. Leonard was told that both the publisher and printer of such a book would be prosecuted; printing so huge a project was unthinkable for their own private press – Virginia estimated in a letter to Weaver that it would take them two years to produce a book of only 300 pages – so they had to decline the opportunity to publish *Ulysses*.[22]

Matters were no more promising in the United States; B. W. Huebsch had brought out the *Portrait* and then all of Joyce's other works as well, but the confiscation of the issues of the *Little Review* had made it clear that it would be impossible to publish *Ulysses*, and after an agonising struggle he regretfully had to inform John Quinn, who was handling things on the American end for Joyce, of his decision (Reid 484–5).

Enter Sylvia Beach.

An American, Beach was five years younger than Joyce; she had made several trips to Europe, including a stay in Paris when her father had taken the family there upon being named associate pastor of the American Church of Paris, and she had spent a year in Florence, before she settled in Paris in 1916. She became a friend and eventually the lover of Adrienne Monnier, the owner of a bookshop, La Maison des Amis des Livres. In 1919 Beach opened her own bookshop and 'lending library', Shakespeare and Company, on the rue Dupuytren; two years later it moved to the rue de l'Odéon, across from Monnier's shop. But to say that Beach owned a bookshop is not in itself fully to convey the importance it and its owner had in the cultural world of Paris in the twenties and thirties, both for Parisians and, especially, for American and British tourists and expatriates. 'Lincoln was a politician', it has been remarked, 'Melville a seaman, Thoreau a camper. She was a bookseller.'[23] And, almost by default, a publisher.

Sylvia Beach had known of Joyce and his work – and 'worshipped' him – before they met one Sunday afternoon in July 1920, at a party at the home of the poet André Spire. She later wrote an evocative and moving description of the meeting and of Joyce himself:

> . . . I strolled into a little room lined to the ceiling with books. There, drooping in a corner between two bookcases, was Joyce.
>
> Trembling, I asked: 'Is this the great James Joyce?'
>
> 'James Joyce,' he replied.
>
> We shook hands; that is, he put his limp, boneless hand in my tough, little paw – if you can call that a handshake.
>
> He was of medium height, thin, slightly stooped, graceful. One noticed his hands. They were very narrow. On the middle and third fingers of the left hand, he wore rings, the stones in heavy settings. His eyes, a deep blue, with the light of genius in them, were extremely beautiful. I noticed, however, that the right eye had a slightly abnormal look and that the right lens of his glasses was thicker than the left. His hair was thick, sandy-colored, wavy, and brushed back from a high, lined forehead over his tall head.
>
> . . .

'What do you do?' Joyce inquired. I told him about Shakespeare and Company. The name, and mine, too, seemed to amuse
him, and a charming smile came to his lips. Taking a small notebook out of his pocket and, as I noticed with sadness, holding it
very close to his eyes, he wrote down the name and address. He
said he would come to see me.

[Beach 34–6]

He began to frequent her shop, and one day in 1921 he came in,
depressed, and gave her an account of the dismal prospects for
publishing *Ulysses* in the US or anywhere: 'My book will never come
out now', he lamented. According to her autobiography, it then
occurred to her to ask, 'Would you let Shakespeare and Company
have the honor of bringing out your *Ulysses*?', and Joyce accepted
'immediately and joyfully' the idea of entrusting his novel 'to such a
funny little publisher' (Beach 47) – or, indeed, would-be publisher,
for she had never yet published anything. The truth may be even
more extreme: it may have been his idea in the first place, for in her
original draft of her memoirs Beach wrote, 'I accepted with enthusiasm Joyce's suggestion that I publish his book' (Fitch 78).

Beach immediately recognised how important such a step could
be for her and her bookshop; as she wrote to her mother, 'Ulysses
means thousands of dollars in publicity for me', and 'Ulysses is
going to make my place famous' (Fitch 78). She was right on both
counts, although the 'thousands of dollars in publicity' did not trans-
late into profits for her personally. She and Joyce had no contract at
this time, but their arrangement was such that Joyce received almost
all the funds that eventually came in from sales. Before publication
she also permitted him seemingly endless revisions and additions in
numerous proofs; she realised that no 'real' publisher could operate
that way (Beach 60), but she provided an exception to the adage that
authors are never geniuses to their publishers.

The printer who had to work with the many proofs and Joyce's
voluminous additions to them – he increased its size by about a third
at this stage (*JJ* 513) – was Maurice Darantiere of Dijon. He and his
employees did a superhuman job considering the many obstacles
(the complexity of the novel, their working in a foreign language, the
constant revisions), but the result was a volume that has produced
textual ambiguities and controversies ever since. Joyce wanted, too,
the cover of *Ulysses* to be in the blue of the Greek flag; finding
precisely the right coloured paper produced further problems and
took Darantiere to Germany (Beach 63).

Beach came up with a plan by which subscriptions to the first printing were ordered in advance; the announcement produced excitement in the literary world, and orders came in from other bookshops in England and the United States, and from publishers, as well as of course from individuals – including Winston Churchill (Fitch 87). The year seemed to be going well for Joyce at last, although he had his doubts: $1 + 9 + 2 + 1$ added up to 13, which led him in his superstition quite seriously to expect 'incessant trouble' from the whole year (*LI* 161). He put great store in symbolic dates and resolved that his novel would appear on his birthday, 2 February, in 1922. On the other hand he did not help matters by continuing to revise proofs drastically, so it was a further sign of Darantiere's diligence and cooperation that, when he was just under the wire and could not trust the post to get the first published volumes in on time, he put two copies on the express train from Dijon to Paris; Beach met it at 7:00 a.m. on 2 February and rushed off by taxi to present Copy No. 1 to Joyce, bringing Copy No. 2 to Shakespeare and Company for display (Beach 84–5).

It was the start of a vintage year in literary history; to mention only works in the English language, 1922 saw the publication not only of *Ulysses* but also of T. S. Eliot's *The Waste Land*, Virginia Woolf's *Jacob's Room*, John Galsworthy's *The Forsyte Saga*, D. H. Lawrence's *Aaron's Rod*, F. Scott Fitzgerald's *The Beautiful and Damned* and Sinclair Lewis's *Babbitt*. None of them, not even *The Waste Land*, came close to causing the stir, at the time or since, that *Ulysses* created. Influential critics in Europe and America praised it as few works are ever hailed; Larbaud, in the extremely prestigious *Nouvelle Revue Française*, claimed that with *Ulysses* 'Ireland is making a sensational re-entrance into high European literature' (in Deming 253). T. S. Eliot had already been profoundly affected, as shown in the tremendous influence of what he had read of the novel on *The Waste Land*. Virginia Woolf, however, as she began to read the published version of the book, was shocked at Eliot's high opinion of it: 'Tom, great Tom, thinks this on a par with War & Peace! An illiterate, underbred book it seems to me: the book of a self taught working man, & we all know how distressing they are, how egotistic, insistent, raw, striking, & ultimately nauseating. When one can have the cooked flesh, why have the raw?' (*Diary*, vol. 2, 189). Yet Woolf's views of Joyce and his accomplishment became much more complex than her initial reactions might have led one to expect. Her response to Joyce always remained ambivalent, but she was also aware of –

and sympathetic towards – much of what he was striving for and achieving.

Ernest Hemingway wrote Sherwood Anderson that 'Joyce has a most goddamn wonderful book', although his enthusiasm for the work could be tempered by a measure of cynicism about the man: 'Meantime the report is that he and all his family are starving', Hemingway continues, 'but you can find the whole celtic crew of them every night in Michaud's where Binney and I can only afford to go about once a week' (*LIII* 55). In time Hemingway was to help smuggle copies into the United States, while for over a decade it became the expected and correct thing for all literate American tourists returning from France to hide a copy somewhere in their luggage. (Many of them must have had problems with the novel's complexities and difficulties, but Joyce, as Margaret Anderson pointed out, had after all gone to the trouble of learning Norwegian in order to read Ibsen, so he was not one to overvalue making things so easy that no effort to read him might be needed [Anderson 248].)

The smuggling was required because the book was considered too scandalous to be published legally in either the United States or England. That was a major problem for Joyce, but he could also be amused by some of the reactions to his novel. The British *Sporting Times*, also called the *Pink 'Un* – a publication with, Joyce relished in claiming, a reputation even worse than his (*DMW* 193) – ran a featured story called 'The Scandal of *Ulysses*' which described the novel as a 'stupid glorification of mere filth' (in Deming 192). Beach put a copy of the paper's poster – prominently displaying the words 'THE SCANDAL OF ULYSSES' – on the wall of her shop, and there is a photograph of Joyce and her posing beneath it. A couple of years later, the recording company His Master's Voice would only agree to record a reading by Joyce from *Ulysses* if the record were made without the company's label and if it would not be listed in their catalogue (Beach 170).

Not all the negative reactions were silly, however. Joyce's family was disturbed, and Aunt Josephine even expressed the opinion that *Ulysses* was not fit to read. Hearing that, Joyce asserted that 'If *Ulysses* isn't fit to read . . . life isn't worth living' (Hutchins 139).

James Joyce was now the infamous author of a notorious book, and the famous writer of a novel acclaimed as a masterpiece. *Ulysses* was published on his fortieth birthday; he was working on its final chapters when he was thirty-eight – the age of Leopold Bloom.

5

Work in Progress: The Years of *Finnegans Wake*, 1922–1941

A gentleman Irish mighty odd.
He had a tongue both rich and sweet. . . .

'Finnegan's Wake' (Irish ballad)

Leave the letter that never begins to go find the latter that ever comes to end, written in smoke and blurred by mist and signed of solitude, sealed at night.

Finnegans Wake (337.11–14)

Ulysses ended with Leopold and Molly Bloom late at night, asleep or about to sleep: for Joyce as for his Shem the Penman in *Finnegans Wake*, 'fame would come . . . twixt a sleep and a wake' (*FW* 192.20). On 10 March 1923 he wrote two pages which he described in a letter to Harriet Shaw Weaver as 'the first I have written since the final *Yes* of *Ulysses*' (*LI* 202), which had been published more than a year earlier; those pages, dealing with the Irish King Roderick O'Conor, provided the inception of the book to which he would devote untold numbers of hours of his creative life during the decades of the 1920s and 1930s: *Finnegans Wake*.

Although the 'basis' of the book, according to Joyce, was an encounter his father had once had with a tramp in Phoenix Park (*LI* 396), a major impulse for it was a desire to do for human existence at night, and in sleep, something like what he had achieved in *Ulysses* for a single day; or, as he reported Stanislaus's exasperation, 'my brother says that having done the longest day in literature I am now conjuring up the darkest night' (*LIII* 140). Such a project demanded an even greater break with traditional literature than his earlier work had represented, for 'one great part of every human existence is passed in a state which cannot be rendered sensible by the use of wideawake language, cutanddry grammar and goahead plot' (*LIII* 146). Indeed for many readers – then and now – the problem is that in the resulting 'Nichtian glossery' what we have may seem to be 'nat language at any sinse of the world' at all (*FW* 83.10–12).

When, in the years during which he worked on the *Wake*, Joyce 'often sighed: I am at the end of English' (*PAE* 64), his remark seems surely to have been as much a boast as a lament. Readers of the *Portrait* had already seen Stephen Dedalus's resentment of the English language in his thoughts during the discussion, with the Dean of Studies, of the word 'tundish':

> The language in which we are speaking is his before it is mine. How different are the words *home, Christ, ale, master,* on his lips and on mine! I cannot speak or write these words without unrest of spirit. His language, so familiar and so foreign, will always be for me an acquired speech. I have not made or accepted its words. My voice holds them at bay. My soul frets in the shadow of his language.
>
> [*P* 189]

Living in exile in cities where English was a foreign tongue – in Pola, Trieste, Rome, Zurich and now in Paris – Joyce felt freer to act on a similar frustration, which he had expressed as early as 1918 while living in Switzerland, when he claimed in a letter that 'writing in English is the most ingenious torture ever devised for sins committed in previous lives' (*LI* 120). It was a torture he eventually supplemented with one even more devilish: for although he did not – like Joseph Conrad for example, or Vladimir Nabokov – adopt a foreign language and cease writing in the language in which he was brought up, he did expand its possibilities and carry it to its limits and beyond.

The James Joyce who felt stifled by the limitations of English could also feel tremendous elation at the seemingly boundless powers offered by *language,* once remarking to Eugene Jolas, 'I have discovered that I can do anything with language I want' (Jolas, 'My Friend' 13). Many readers agree, and few would deny that he showed himself willing to try, although to some the result seemed almost insane, an accusation Joyce himself could sometimes understand; he is reported to have told a friend:

And perhaps it is madness to grind up words in order to extract their substance, or to graft one onto another, to create cross-breeds and unknown variants, to open up unsuspected possibilities for these words, to marry sounds which were not usually joined before, although they were meant for one another, to allow water to speak like water, birds to chirp in the words of birds, to liberate all sounds of rustling, breaking, arguing, shouting, cracking, whistling, creaking, gurgling – from their servile, contemptible role and to attach them to the feelers of expressions which grope for definitions of the undefined.

[Parandowski, in *PAE* 160]

As such an impassioned exclamation suggests, the language of *Finnegans Wake* is not merely 'anythongue athall' (*FW* 117.15–16) but rather a fascinating, intense, even magnificent exploration of the possibilities of human communication. Major elements of that exploration are puns and 'portmanteau' words: as when, in a self-reflexive moment in the book, one character asks another, 'Are we speachin d'anglas landage or are you sprakin sea Djoytsch?' (*FW* 485.12–13) – a sentence which, without exhausting its possible significations, uses both French (*d'anglais*) and German (*sprechen Sie Deutsch?*) to wonder if the language the book uses is 'English' or 'Joyce'. Similarly, when the *Wake* refers to 'the book of Doublends Jined' (*FW* 20.15–16), among the items packed into that portmanteau are references to Dublin's giant (and his avatars Finn, Finnegan, HCE, and others) and to the fact that the book's 'ends' – its start and its finish – are joined, as the last word, 'the', seems to bring us back around to the first word, 'riverrun'.

The book's ambition is immense in numerous ways. Once, when asked by Harriet Shaw Weaver what he would work on after *Ulysses*, he replied that he thought he would 'write a history of the world' (*DMW* 203). That history is evoked through what the *Wake* calls the 'monomyth' (*FW* 581.24), in which many – sometimes the effect seems to be that all – of the world's myths, legends, folklore and historical events are evoked through the figures of a single family living in Chapelizod, near Dublin: the husband and father, HCE (Humphrey Chimpden Earwicker); the wife and mother, ALP (Anna Livia Plurabelle); and their two sons (Shem, similar in some key ways to Joyce himself, and Shaun, often reminiscent of Stanislaus); and their daughter (Issy). An important grounding for the presentation of the monomyth was the thought of the eighteenth-century

Italian philosopher and historian, Giambattista Vico, who believed that the study of both language and mythology can illuminate the course of history, which is thereby revealed to occur and recur in cycles. As the *Wake* puts it, history 'moves in vicous cicles yet remews the same': 'the seim anew. Ordovico or viricordo. Anna was, Livia is, Plurabelle's to be' (134.16–17; 215.23–4). Joyce clearly found Vico's ideas stimulating and valuable, although he usually hedged when discussing how 'seriously' he took them, as when he wrote to Weaver that 'I would not pay overmuch attention to these theories, beyond using them for all they are worth, but they have gradually forced themselves on me through circumstances of my own life' (*LI* 241; interestingly, he immediately adds, 'I wonder where Vico got his fear of thunderstorms').

The title itself reflects both Joyce's methods and his themes: the Irish-American ballad 'Finnegan's Wake' (with the apostrophe) tells of the fall and death of a hod carrier, Tim Finnegan, who turns out not to be dead after all, rising up – awakening – during a free-for-all fight at his wake. Without the apostrophe, Joyce suggests that all Finnegans shall awake, and that their counterpart the Irish mythical hero Finn MacCool shall awake again. The title meant so much to him that he kept it secret until the publication of his work in book form in 1939; until then, he told only Nora its actual title, publishing excerpts as *Work in Progress*.

If all that sounds like a mere 'game', Joyce was not unaware of such a possible accusation; he wrote to Weaver in 1926, after several years of work on his book, that 'I know it is no more than a game but it is a game that I have learned to play in my own way. Children may just as well play as not. The ogre will come in any case' (*LIII* 144). Actually, above all he wished *Finnegans Wake* to be seen as *fun* – the wake as a *'funferal'* (*FW* 120.10). If he expressed his ironic intention, as we have seen, to keep the professors busy for centuries, he would also provide the academy of letters with 'acomedy of letters' (*FW* 425.24). Yet he was also fully aware – how could he not be? – of the demands he was making on his readers, and of the difficulty of his massive work; he once told Nino Frank, in regard to their task of translating a section of the *Wake* into Italian, that they must not delay: 'for the moment there is at least one person, myself, who can understand what I am writing. I don't however guarantee that in two or three years I'll still be able to' (*JJ* 700). It is no wonder then that within the *Wake* itself, just after using the word *'funferal'*, he refers to 'that ideal reader suffering from an ideal insomnia' (*FW* 120.13–14).

Nor is it any wonder that some less than 'ideal' readers were, from the start, less than completely receptive to the *Wake*. Joyce wrote to Weaver that he was 'more and more aware of the indignant hostility shown to my experiment in interpreting "the dark night of the soul"' (*LI* 258); 'hostility' is not too strong a term. A number of readers who had already begun to have reservations about the latter sections of *Ulysses* lost much or all of their patience with *Work in Progress* – including Stanislaus and even Ezra Pound, who memorably avowed to Joyce that he could 'make nothing of it whatever. Nothing so far as I make out, nothing short of divine vision or a new cure for the clapp can possibly be worth all the circumambient peripherization' (*LIII* 145). Others who had been enthusiastic about Joyce's earlier work tried to keep their reservations to themselves, like Stuart Gilbert, who reflected in his diary that what Joyce 'is doing is too easy to do, and too hard to understand (for the reader)' (Gilbert, 'Selections' 17). Mary Colum, perhaps more honest, told Joyce that his new work was 'outside literature'.[1] H. G. Wells wrote Joyce a thoughtful letter in which he recognised that the new 'literary experiment' was:

> . . . a considerable thing because you are a very considerable man and you have in your composition a mighty genius for expression which has escaped discipline. But I don't think it gets anywhere. You have turned your back on common men, on their elementary needs and their restricted time and intelligence. . . .
> . . . It has its believers and its following. Let them rejoice in it. To me it is a dead end.
>
> [*LI* 275]

In the face of such responses, Joyce needed encouragement, of the sort for which he had come to rely a great deal on Harriet Shaw Weaver; so he was particularly devastated when she too could no longer hold back her reservations about the directions of his new artistic departures.

In January 1927 she wrote to confess 'that I do not care much for the output from your Wholesale Safety Pun Factory nor for the darkness and the unintelligibilities of your deliberately-entangled language system'. She echoed what many others must have felt when she went on to say that 'it seems to me you are wasting your genius'. She then told him not to pay too much attention to her comments: 'I daresay I am wrong.' Joyce was so disturbed by her letter that he took to bed for several days in a kind of collapse.[2]

In his discouragement, Joyce even thought of the unlikely scenario that someone else might finish the book for him. In May 1927 he wrote to Weaver that he had hit upon the selection of the Dublin novelist and poet James Stephens, although Joyce averred that 'of course he would never take a fraction of the time or pains I take but so much the better for him and me and possibly for the book itself'; he enjoyed the possibility that 'JJ and S (the colloquial Irish for John Jameson and Son's Dublin whisky) would be a nice lettering under the title' (*LI* 253–4). He became even more intrigued when he heard that Stephens and he shared precisely the same birthday, no small factor in Joyce's cosmology; he persisted in his notion and in 1929 reported to Weaver that Stephens was 'much impressed and moved by my proposal to hand over the work to him' but had assured Joyce that there would be no need for anyone else to take the job on, and that the 'Anna Livia Plurabelle' section of the *Wake* was 'the greatest prose ever written by a man' – an interesting turn-around from someone who had written to John Quinn in 1917, 'I don't like Joyce's work, but he can write'.[3]

Ulysses, too, even after its publication, continued to generate problems. Its publication and importation continued to be illegal in the United States, which also left it in at best an uncertain legal position in regard to copyright. Taking advantage of that situation, an American publisher, Samuel Roth, began in 1926 to publish – without Joyce's permission – expurgated versions of the novel in serial form, in his review *Two Worlds Monthly*. Joyce engaged some attorneys for the ponderous process of legal action, but in the meantime he also encouraged an international protest signed by a great many of the world's most prominent literary figures. Once again he followed his instinct about the importance of dates and arranged for the protest to be dated 2 February 1927; carefully avoiding a position on whether the exclusion of the novel from the United States was justified, the statement appealed 'to the American public in the name of that security of works of the intellect and the imagination without which art cannot live, to oppose to Mr. Roth's enterprise the full power of honorable and fair opinion' (*LIII* 152). Joyce was gratified at the number of writers who signed, although a stubborn refusal came from Ezra Pound, who would have preferred an all-out attack on 'the infamous state of the American law' and 'the whole American people which sanction the state of the laws' (Pound 226). According to Joyce's report Ernest Hemingway assured him 'this was moonshine as it would do me no end of harm with thousands of Americans who had supported me and support me still'; in any case Joyce 'had not for a moment the faintest intention' of taking Pound's advice (*SL* 342).

The letter was signed by 167 writers. Some signatures, of people in Joyce's circle in one way or another, were to be expected: Édouard Dujardin, Eugene Jolas, Italo Svevo and others. Some, like the names of Ernest Hemingway, Rebecca West and Thornton Wilder, provided notable testimony from a younger generation of writers. Joyce would inevitably have noted the signatures of a number of Irish authors: Sean O'Casey, Liam O'Flaherty, AE, James Stephens, and no doubt above all William Butler Yeats. A few names of especially prominent figures must have provided particular gratification: Albert Einstein, for example, or Maurice Maeterlinck and Thomas Mann. Perhaps most interesting is the fact that the letter was also signed by some of Joyce's contemporaries who had their own grave reservations about *Ulysses* and even about its morality – such as E. M. Forster, D. H. Lawrence and Virginia Woolf.

Gratifying as the protest was, it had little practical effect, and Roth did not cease publication of the serial portions of his expurgated *Ulysses* until an injunction forced him to do so in December 1928 (*JJ* 587), although he somehow still managed to publish his own pirated version in book form in 1929.

Joyce also began to have difficulties with his official publisher, Sylvia Beach. Their financial arrangement had always been informal at best, distinctly to Joyce's advantage; but in the late 1920s and early 1930s, as chances increased for the successful publication of legitimate editions of *Ulysses* in addition to – or even instead of – that of Shakespeare and Company, their relationship became strained. Beach felt that any edition published in the United States would kill the sales of hers, and that that would mean – Joyce reported to Weaver – 'shutting her shop and rearing chickens but that she would do it if it was my wish' (*LIII* 230). Beach and Joyce both tried valiantly to keep on cordial terms, but Adrienne Monnier, furious over the way she felt her friend and companion had been treated, and fully aware of the genuine financial difficulties Beach was now facing, wrote Joyce a letter in May 1931 accusing him of having taken advantage of Beach and of being much more concerned with money than the world realised (*JJ* 651). In later years Beach too, in a passage in an early draft of her memoir which she excised before publication, wrote that she had begun to see Joyce 'in another light': 'not only as a very great writer but also as a great business man, hard as nails' (in Fitch 326).

As negotiations began about the possibility of other editions, Beach grew concerned when it became evident that *Ulysses* was being treated as if it were still in manuscript rather than as a book she had published and had been selling for almost a decade; she later wrote that it had not occurred to her that she might profit from a new edition 'until I realized that it hadn't occurred to anyone else. Then I began to be exasperated at being ignored' (Beach 202). It was not until the end of 1930 that Joyce and Beach even signed a formal contract, in which she was awarded exclusive rights to *Ulysses* 'throughout the world', until they might both agree that it was in his best interests for the rights to be sold by her 'at the price set by herself'; in the meantime, Joyce would be paid the extraordinary royalty of twenty-five per cent (Beach 203).

The next year, 1931, decisions about what she would be recompensed if another edition were published had to be faced: her demand turned out to be the immense sum, for the time, of $25 000 (Fitch 317). No one could deny, then or now, that she fully deserved even such a high figure, given all that she had done – and all the financial sacrifices she had made for Joyce over a number of years; nevertheless, no publisher could have agreed to such a demand, and matters stalled for a time. Finally Padraic Colum acted as an intermediary, making periodic visits to Shakespeare and Company on Joyce's behalf; one day he asked her what rights she had to *Ulysses*, and she mentioned that after all there was her contract. When he doubted its existence and she showed it to him, he at last blurted out the message that, she later said, 'immediately floored me': 'You are standing in Joyce's way!' As soon as he left, Beach telephoned Joyce and in cool anger told him that she would make 'no further claims' on *Ulysses*.[4] In fact, however, she did obtain royalties from some editions, and Joyce had also presented her, in gratitude, with the manuscript of *Stephen Hero*.

Yet it is fully clear that until then, over the years, she had made little or no profit from being the publisher of *Ulysses*; Joyce was aware of all he owed to her, and when, during the disagreements about the transfer of rights, someone criticised Sylvia Beach's behaviour, in his presence, he replied that 'all she did was to make me a present of the ten best years of her life'. Her life was surely not quite so totally devoted to his as such a remark presumes, but in the late

1950s she was deeply moved to hear that comment reported to her (Jolas, 'The Joyce I Knew' 86). In her memoir, Beach admits to having been 'not at all proud' of her own 'personal feelings' in regard to the resolution of all the negotiations, and then adds, 'after all, the books were Joyce's. A baby belongs to its mother, not to the midwife, doesn't it?' (Beach 205) – a metaphor which may seem ironic in retrospect, given the probable importance her being a woman had in the way her role as the original and for a decade the sole publisher of *Ulysses* was in key ways ignored. As she wrote to her sister, 'it must be because of my sex that they think I wouldn't charge them anything' (Fitch 318); Harriet Shaw Weaver – herself a publisher – tempered her ordinarily total loyalty to Joyce by writing to Beach, 'I understand your desire and determination to make all these men publishers recognise your rights and position as first (and most courageous and enterprising and hardworking) publisher of Mr Joyce's wonderful book' (*DMW* 307).

The intensity of the interest in publishing *Ulysses* was a result of the growing fame both the novel and its author had attained over the decade of the 1920s, by the end of which James Joyce – certainly not the most widely read of authors in the English language – was probably the most famous. He was also coming to be extremely influential, especially it seemed on many of the younger American novelists, despite the fact that his most famous book was still banned in their country. Some of them, on visits to Europe – like William Faulkner and Thomas Wolfe – stood aside in awe as they stared at their hero, unable to gather the courage to speak to him. Even best-selling authors like Hemingway and F. Scott Fitzgerald recognised Joyce's special standing. And one day during the 1930s, at the elegant and celebrity-haunted restaurant Fouquet's in Paris, the German novelist Erich Maria Remarque, the author of the hugely successful *All Quiet on the Western Front* (1929), was with Marlene Dietrich waiting for a table when they struck up a conversation with Mary Colum, who introduced them to her companion. When she mentioned 'Monsieur James Joyce', the 'effect was electrical', and both the movie star and the author were obviously excited; Joyce was amused and clearly pleased (Colum 148).

As the author of a banned book, Joyce was notorious as well as eminent. Sylvia Beach probably has a valid point when she reflects, 'Actually, I think the banning of *Ulysses* was a fortunate thing. So great a writer might otherwise have waited several hundred years to become famous except in the comparatively small group that will go in for a *Ulysses*' (Beach 189).

Harriet Shaw Weaver made the first attempt to publish a British edition in 1922, when she arranged for the poet, translator and publisher John Rodker to be in charge of an Egoist Press edition utilising the sheets of the Shakespeare and Company edition; two thousand copies were printed in Dijon in October (they indicated that they had been 'Published for the Egoist Press, London by John Rodker, Paris 1922'). For more than a year Weaver sold copies in London and by post with a great deal of quiet discretion; her efforts came to an end, however, when the Customs at Folkestone seized a shipment of a second printing of five hundred copies in early 1923. Weaver decided not to contest the seizure in court, and as a result the books were destroyed, probably burned (*DMW* 203–17).

But by the early thirties the climate seemed to be changing in regard to possible publication in the United States (the book was already being taught in American universities and copies could be found in university libraries, banned or not), and publishing firms became serious in their negotiations for the novel. The winning bid was submitted by Bennett Cerf, who came to Paris in 1932 and negotiated the contract in person; Cerf had started the firm of Random House in his twenties, after purchasing the Modern Library series from Horace Liveright. Not everyone was happy that Joyce had accepted Cerf's offer out of the several possibilities; as Stuart Gilbert wrote in his diary, there was some concern that Joyce had chosen a publisher who was Jewish: 'Colums rather sick about it; they had found a Christian publisher and believe that there would be a better chance of getting past the censorship if a Jew (and one who, it seems, had a name for publishing outrageous books) were not to sponsor *Ulysses*' (Gilbert, 'Selections' 23–4).

In fact Joyce knew what he was doing, and so did Cerf, who turned out to be extremely adept at guiding the book through the intricate and controversial tangles of making its publication legal in the US. Most shrewdly of all, perhaps, he chose Morris L. Ernst to be the attorney in charge of the case. Ernst had already become well known in the realm of censorship and the law, and he had co-authored a book on the topic, *To the Pure*, in 1928; the year after that he defended Radclyffe Hall's novel about homosexuality, *The Well of Loneliness*; by 1931 he had already thought of taking part in a case involving *Ulysses*, writing in a private memo to his partner that 'it would be the grandest case in the history of law and literature, and I am ready to do anything in the world to get it started' (Stevens 92).

One clever move was aimed at making it possible to get into the court records opinions about the novel by eminent literary figures and critics; ordinarily such external opinions were ruled irrelevant. So Random House took one of the copies of the Paris edition they had in the US and pasted into it all the quotations they wanted to use (with comments by, for example, the poet William Rose Benét, the philosopher John Dewey, the publisher Alfred A. Knopf, the critics Edmund Wilson and Malcolm Cowley, the editor and writer H. L. Mencken, and the novelists Theodore Dreiser and John Cowper Powys). They sent the bulging volume back to Europe – and then had someone bring it back by ship, so that it would be that particular copy which would be seized, making all the pasted-in quotations admissible at the trial. Cerf's representative was at the dock when the ship arrived; because of a heat wave the Customs officers wanted no delays and were letting everyone go through without inspections. The Random House agent, however, stubbornly insisted that the relevant bag be opened; when an exasperated officer searched it and saw the copy of *Ulysses*, he simply said, 'Oh, for God's sake, everybody brings that in. We don't pay any attention to it'. It was only at the insistence of the Random House representative, and with the authority of the officer's supervisor, that the United States Customs did in fact seize the book (Cerf 92–3).

The Chief Assistant US Attorney in charge of the government's case against *Ulysses*, Samuel C. Coleman, also seems to have been reluctant and a bit discomfited in regard to his duties; a memo from Ernst mentioned in July 1932 that Coleman had read the novel and 'thought that it was a literary masterpiece, but that it was obscene within the meaning of the federal law'; Coleman even encouraged 'passing *Ulysses* around in the United States Attorney's office. He said that that was the only way his staff would get a literary education' (in Moscato 157). When, during the trial, Ernst's wife attended, Coleman mentioned to Ernst that he was too embarrassed to read aloud in her presence, as he had intended, some of the 'obscene' passages from the novel (Stevens 100).

Coleman and Ernst agreed that a jury trial would entail reading the entire novel aloud in court, so instead the trial was heard before a judge; Ernst was successful in his desire to have that judge be John M. Woolsey, known to be a literate man. He also clearly had some wit. When, during the proceedings, Ernst defended the word 'fuck' as more honest than other phrases used 'to connote the same experience', and Woolsey asked for an example, Ernst suggested '"they slept together." It means the same thing.' Smiling, Woolsey said, 'That isn't even usually the truth'. At that moment, Ernst has said, he 'knew that the case was half won' (Ernst 22).

Woolsey's opinion was handed down 6 December 1933, in favour of publication; it was a landmark decision in the history of censorship in the United States. He wrote that 'in "Ulysses", in spite of its unusual frankness, I do not detect anywhere the leer of the sensualist', and that 'whilst in many places the effect of "Ulysses" on the reader undoubtedly is somewhat emetic, no where does it tend to be an aphrodisiac.'[5] (The statement Joyce subsequently authorised for release to the press remarked that he found the judge 'to be not devoid of a sense of humour' [*JJ* 667].) Even Assistant US Attorney Coleman agreed that 'the result is, I think, a wholesome one. I welcome the decision and am satisfied with it'; his superior, the US Attorney Martin Conboy, disagreed, and appealed; Woolsey's decision was upheld in the Circuit Court of Appeals, two to one (interestingly, the dissenting justice – who based his opinion on morality – was later convicted and imprisoned for corruption).[6] There were headlines all over the country (*Time* put Joyce on its cover), and immediately the book sold well: it was published in January 1934 and sold 35 000 copies by mid-April, more than it had ever sold in all the years of the Shakespeare and Company edition (Fitch 342). Morris Ernst, who had agreed to take on the case for the very low fee of $500, with the stipulation that if successful he would earn royalties from the publication of *Ulysses* for the rest of his life, subsequently earned a small fortune for his efforts; the book, Cerf has testified, was also his first 'really important trade publication' and 'did a lot for Random House' (Cerf 92–3).

In the meantime, the Odyssey Press in Germany had published its English-language edition in December 1932 (the last printing of the Shakespeare and Company edition, the eleventh, having appeared in May 1930); the first unsuppressed British edition, published by John Lane, did not appear until October 1936.

The passing years and, in particular, the responses to *Work in Progress* brought about new patterns in Joyce's friendships. He saw Budgen only rarely, and with Pound and Beach his relationship was never again close. Weaver remained as loyal as always, but otherwise he and Nora began to form new friendships – for example with young American writers such as the poet, novelist and short story writer Robert McAlmon, whose memoir *Being Geniuses Together* (1938) presents a vividly subjective portrait of the Paris of the 1920s.

Especially notable were Joyce's friendships with some of the most influential literary figures in the France of his time. Valery Larbaud was already a prominent novelist when his *Amants, heureux amants* appeared in 1923, heavily influenced by *Ulysses*, of which he went on to be one of the translators into French; in late 1921, shortly before the publication of *Ulysses*, he introduced it and Joyce to the French literary scene with a well-publicised and well-attended lecture at Adrienne Monnier's bookshop, La Maison des Amis de Livres. Louis Gillet, a member of the French Academy and a critic for the immensely prestigious and traditional *Revue des Deux Mondes*, published a fairly negative article about *Ulysses* in that journal in 1925; but by the early 1930s he 'began discerning the greatness of the phenomenon *Ulysses*' (Gillet, *PAE* 177), becoming an active as well as distinguished champion of Joyce's work, and a good friend.

No friendships were nearly so important to Joyce as his family, but Gillet and others have testified to the significance he placed on social gatherings, especially when they entailed birthdays, name-days, anniversaries or otherwise sacred dates. Often those occasions were celebrated at restaurants – always fine ones, usually expensive – but parties at the Joyce home were also common. They generally took a regular pattern of dinner, followed by music and songs at the piano. One friend, the Surrealist writer Philippe Soupault, confesses to occasional frustration at 'the slightly monotonous nature' of these gatherings but reports that 'it wouldn't do to try leaving the party before its finish, that is to say around three or four o'clock in the morning' (Soupault, *PAE* 114). Occasionally Joyce himself would dance a jig; once, after he had done so to 'Auld Lang Syne' at a New Year's Eve party, Nora remarked that he was 'making a fool of himself' and made everyone leave; Stuart Gilbert, reporting that event in his diary, disagreed with Nora and described Joyce as 'a nimble dancer' (Gilbert, 'Selections' 15).

Less positively, Gilbert recorded feeling 'up to the neck' in the 'muddy intrigues' of some of Joyce's circle, while Harold Nicolson wrote in his diary in 1934 of his sense, upon meeting Joyce, 'that he is surrounded with a group of worshippers and that he has little contact with reality'.[7] There is no doubt that Joyce expected a great deal of his friends: above all he demanded loyalty in their attitudes toward himself and his family – and his work. Nino Frank reports reading the French translation of *Ulysses* and feeling like 'an ill-prepared student with an exam to take, and I dreaded the fatal day when I was certain that I would have to give the author a report on my reading in order to receive a place in the army of followers' (*PAE* 84).

For his part, Joyce was no less loyal to his friends; according to Maria Jolas, 'he had a talent for friendship that was quite extra-ordinary, and I believe that this was one of the reasons why he didn't give his friendship very easily; it was a responsibility for him' (in Kain, 'Interview' 95–6). Eugene and Maria Jolas were an American couple living in Paris who came to know and be intimate with the Joyces in 1926. They founded the magazine *transition*, in which Eugene Jolas published his 'manifesto' on 'The Revolution of the Word' in 1929, an essay revealing attitudes toward the revolution of language which showed great receptivity toward the kind of experiments Joyce was performing in *Work in Progress*. By April 1927, in fact, *transition* had begun publishing that work in instalments, which appeared – sporadically – until 1938, the year before the appearance of *Finnegans Wake*.

Mary Colum also provides a sense of the seriousness with which Joyce took his friendships:

> Joyce had devoted friends: he was a reliable friend himself, and would help one with any old thing – with finding an apartment or a maid or a doctor, with planning a journey or picking out a hotel. If one of his friends was ill, he would shower him with attentions – principally bottles of wine. When we were in Paris he would telephone every day to find out how we were and how things were going with us. On the other side of it, Joyce expected a lot of attention from those he knew, and, on account of his eyes, a great deal of help.

[Colum 123]

An Irish friend of Joyce (and of Samuel Beckett), Thomas McGreevy (who later spelled his name MacGreevy), reports that, while he lived in Paris, if his concierge summoned him in the morning it would as likely as not 'be Joyce wanting something or other that had suggested itself to him as a result of the previous evening's talk' – although often Nora 'would save me the trouble: "Don't mind him, Tom. If God himself came down from Heaven that fellow would find something for him to do. . . ."' (in Dawson 312).

Among the most significant tasks his friends might perform was translating Joyce's work. Larbaud supervised and reviewed the translation of *Ulysses* into French, which was done primarily by Auguste Morel with many suggestions by Joyce himself and important revisions and editing by another new friend, Stuart Gilbert. A British civil servant who had retired early from the Burmese service and now lived in Paris, Gilbert also began a critical book explicating *Ulysses*; Joyce fully cooperated in the project, often providing Gilbert with hints in the form of suggestions of what he might read (*JJ* 600–1); *James Joyce's Ulysses: A Study* appeared in 1931, while the novel was in fact still banned in the United States and England.

The first book-length study of Joyce's work had appeared in 1924: Herbert Gorman's *James Joyce: His First Forty Years*. Gorman also lived in Paris, and Joyce chose him to write an official biography – although Joyce was frustrated at the delay in its completion, as well as determined that it not be overly revealing (*JJ* 666, 726); Gorman's *James Joyce* appeared in 1940. Meanwhile, another friend, Frank Budgen, published *James Joyce and the Making of Ulysses* – a still useful and very readable memoir – in 1934.

A whole group of friends and acquaintances – twelve in all – cooperated with Joyce in producing a collection of essays designed to elucidate, publicise and to some degree make palatable the complex work in which he was engaged during these years. *Our Exagmination Round His Factification for Incamination of Work in Progress* appeared in 1929, the last Joyce publication by Shakespeare and Company. Joyce was intimately involved in its conception and execution – according to his own testimony, standing 'behind those twelve Marshals more or less directing them what lines of research to follow' (*LI* 283); the twelve were Samuel Beckett (whose essay on the roles of Dante, Bruno and Vico in *Work in Progress* was particularly important), Marcel Brion, Frank Budgen, Stuart Gilbert, Eugene Jolas, Victor Llona, Robert McAlmon, Thomas McGreevy, Elliot Paul, John Rodker (Harriet Shaw Weaver's co-publisher of the aborted British edition of *Ulysses*), Robert Sage, and William Carlos Williams.

Beckett had met Joyce the year before, 1928, through McGreevy (Bair 67); he had already read and profoundly admired *Ulysses*. Joyce in turn recognised – sooner than the rest of the world – that 'he has talent' (*LIII* 316), and he once gratified Beckett by quoting from memory a passage from *Murphy* (*JJ* 701). Beckett performed so many services for Joyce that for a long time the story went around that he was Joyce's 'secretary'; but while Beckett, like so many others, did errands or read for him and to him, the younger Irishman was never anything so formal as Joyce's secretary (Bair 71). Beckett recorded his deep feelings for Joyce in many ways, including a late short play, *Ohio Impromptu*, in which a Reader reads aloud to a Listener descriptions of walks on the Isle of Swans in Paris, where Beckett and Joyce used to walk together; other hints – such as the mention of the 'Latin Quarter hat' the young Joyce had worn in Paris and which also appears in *Ulysses* – connect Joyce to the figure being described as one of two people who 'grew to be as one' (Beckett, *Three Plays* 13, 17).

Of course some of the writers with whom Joyce came in contact were, unlike Beckett, already well known – T. S. Eliot, for example, whose *The Waste Land* was profoundly influenced by what he had read of *Ulysses*. Joyce, in a 1925 letter to Weaver, repaid the compliment with a clever parody of Eliot's poem, recounting his holiday travels and beginning, '*Rouen is the rainiest place*', going on to complain, '*I heard mosquitoes swarm in old Bordeaux/ So many!/ I had not thought the earth contained so many*', and concluding, '*But we shall have great times/ When we return to Clinic, that waste land/ O Esculapios!/ (Shan't we? Shan't we? Shan't we?)*' (LI 231).

Joyce's relationship with still another expatriate American, Gertrude Stein, was much more distant. Stein resented the attention Joyce received in Paris, where she felt she should reign supreme, especially given her sense of a prior claim to literary eminence through her experimental work of fiction *Three Lives* (1909); the two met only once, in 1930, and had very little to say to each other on the occasion (Benstock, *Women* 16–18, 457).

The sole encounter between James Joyce and Marcel Proust was apparently no more spectacularly productive. Some accounts of their meeting claim that it was quite brief (for example, 'I regret that I don't know Mr. Joyce's work, said Proust./ I have never read Mr. Proust, said Joyce' [Anderson, *My Thirty Years' War* 245]), while other versions – no doubt equally exaggerated – indicate that the two got along very well once literary matters were put aside. According to Ford Madox Ford's account, their various admirers placed them in chairs and set themselves around the two men, eagerly awaiting their conversation; Proust began by referring to his *Du côté de chez Swann* with the expectation that of course Joyce had read it; Joyce however confessed that he had not and then mentioned Mr. Bloom, assuming Proust had read *Ulysses*, but Proust replied '*Mais, non, monsieur*':

Service fell again to M. Proust. He apologised for the lateness of his arrival. He said it was due to a malady of the liver. He detailed clearly and with minuteness the symptoms of his illness.

'. . . *Tiens, monsieur*', Joyce interrupted. 'I have almost exactly the same symptoms. Only in my case the analysis . . .'

So till eight next morning, in perfect amity and enthusiasm, surrounded by the awed faithful they discussed their maladies.

[Ford 293–4]

A striking example of Joyce's willingness to go to extreme lengths to be helpful to friends is provided by his campaign on behalf of the Irish tenor John Sullivan, whom he had first met in Zurich and then again in 1929 when Sullivan came to sing at the Paris Opera (*JJ* 619). Joyce used to say, 'I don't like music . . . I like singing' (*PAE* 195); or, as he wrote to Weaver in 1930: 'I have always insisted that I know little about literature, less about music, nothing about painting and less than nothing about sculpture; but I do know something about singing, I think.' Caring passionately about that art, he admired his countryman's voice a great deal, as 'incomparably the greatest human voice I have ever heard' (*LI* 291). Joyce claimed that he had gone through the score of *Guillaume Tell*, the opera in which he felt Sullivan especially excelled, and discovered 'that Sullivan sings 456 G's, 93 A flats, 92 A's, 54 B flats, 15 B's, 19 C's, and 2 C sharps. Nobody else can do it' (in Gorman 346).

Clearly, too, he saw in Sullivan a man who had taken as a career one that he had himself contemplated; his description of Sullivan could be in a number of particulars – pro and con – a self-portrait as well: 'In temperament he is intractable, quarrelsome, disconnected, contemptuous, inclined to bullying, undiplomatic, but on the other hand good humoured, sociable, unaffected, amusing and well-informed' (*LI* 290). Above all, perhaps, Sullivan saw himself as the persecuted victim of a conspiracy to thwart his talent in favour of Italian singers, a view of human existence which Joyce never hesitated to share. (Gilbert wrote in his diary about Joyce, 'To fill his life he pictures himself as a victim pursued by enemies, and will not understand that most people are indifferent – e.g., "*le cas Sullivan*" – neither for, nor against', and noted his own impression that, in Sullivan, Joyce saw 'what he would like to have been' ['Selections' 24, 14].) In the revealingly titled 'From a Banned Writer to a Banned Singer', a *Wake*-like piece he published in 1932 as part of his campaign on Sullivan's behalf, Joyce wrote: 'Just out of kerryosity

[Sullivan was from County Kerry] howlike is a Sullivan? It has the fortefaccia of a Markus Brutas, the wingthud of a spread-eagle, the body uniformed of a metropoliceman with the brass feet of a collared grand' (*CW* 259).

For several years Joyce spent so much time on Sullivan's cause – getting notices in the papers, arranging for favourable crowds to attend Sullivan's engagements, writing numerous letters – that many of his friends felt he was carrying things much too far, even to neglecting his own work; Joyce recognised that people were beginning to wonder if he 'had gone slightly soft in the head' (*LI* 291). Once, after medical attention had improved his vision, he went to a production of *Guillaume Tell* in which Sullivan was singing and, during a dramatic moment, took off dark glasses and loudly claimed that the performance had restored his sight after twenty years, shouting '*Merci, mon Dieu, pour ce miracle. Après vingt ans, je revois la lumière*'. Unfortunately, all Joyce's efforts could not make Sullivan a major star, probably because by the time the two men became friends, Sullivan's voice was already – by his own testimony – in decline (*JJ* 624, 698).

The Joyce who was capable of such intense loyalty could also inspire it, as we have seen. Although often in his life those who devoted themselves to his well-being and his art were women, during the last decade of Joyce's life perhaps the most notable and moving of such friendships was with a Russian Jewish émigré with a name Joyce could only regard as a fitting omen, given its closeness to that of the hero of *Ulysses*, Leopold Paula Bloom: Paul Leopoldovitch Léon. Léon and his wife Lucie (who wrote under the name Lucie Noel) had fled the Bolsheviks in 1918; his brother Alex – who also knew Helen Kastor Fleischman, the woman Giorgio Joyce would eventually marry – had been giving Joyce Russian lessons, and through those connections Joyce and Léon met in 1928. Léon had been trained in law (having written a thesis on Irish Home Rule [Nadel 227]) and was a highly cultured person; as his wife reports, 'He was a scholar with a knowledge of Greek and Latin, and a professor of philosophy and sociology. His special studies were Rousseau and Benjamin Constant. He was secretary of the journal, *International Archives of Sociology* and was active in the Society of Sociologists and Philosophers' (Noel 7).

Léon was twelve years younger than Joyce, and in fact in some ways became as close to Giorgio as to Joyce himself, but given Joyce's deep family feelings, that tie in fact helped to make their

bond closer. Léon took over many of the business duties formerly
assumed by Sylvia Beach and went beyond them, writing letters,
arranging or avoiding meetings, in some ways acting as a literary
agent, providing legal advice, and performing numerous other tasks
– all without any payment whatsoever. As with Beckett, although
his duties for Joyce were much more varied, time-consuming and
prolonged, he was never a 'secretary' and resented being regarded
as such.[8]

It cannot have been easy handling the affairs of a man like Joyce
– especially the financial ones. He and Nora almost invariably dined
out, and never at budget restaurants; Joyce often insisted on picking
up the tab for any group of which he was a part, and he was a
generous tipper; when the family went on holiday, they always
stayed at luxury hotels; as Beach puts it, the Joyces urged the Gilberts
to stay at 'the local Palace Hotel. Mr. Gilbert said he couldn't afford
to. Neither could the Joyces' (Beach 197). They also dressed very
well: Nora had become clothes-conscious, and there was even a note
of dandyism in Joyce's dress.[9] Moreover, as we shall see, Lucia's
illness became a major drain on the family finances.

Joyce complained that his income did not come near matching
Picasso's, who 'has not a higher name than I have' but who could
'get 20,000 or 30,000 francs for a few hours' work' (*LI* 258); during the
1920s Joyce's royalties were in truth minimal (in 1924 he reported
that 'in one year not a single copy of *A Portrait of the Artist* has been
sold in the United States' [*LIII* 95]). But that situation changed drastically with the publication of the Random House edition of *Ulysses*.
Prior to that (and afterward, for that matter), there were the substantial amounts provided by Harriet Shaw Weaver. Joyce constantly
had to request permission to draw upon the principal, as well as the
income, from those gifts, causing consternation in Weaver's solicitors. The amounts reflected in Weaver's gifts were in fact extremely
substantial; over the years, they probably came to close to half a
million pounds in current values.[10] Yet it is perhaps appropriate to
keep in mind that – as Weaver's biographers have argued – the
amounts involved would, on a yearly basis, 'not seem exorbitant to
any professional man who was obliged to pay for doctors, medicine
and his children's education'. Still, the expenses were for a family
not Weaver's own, and for a 'professional man' who lived more
luxuriously in many ways than she herself did, so her generosity is
all the more notable, and her insistence on the importance of Joyce's
independence all the more admirable. Some of Joyce's friends and

acquaintances felt that, given Joyce's propensities for extravagance, Weaver would have been wiser to have refrained from providing him any capital, and that she should have chosen instead to award him a yearly income; but, as those same biographers also argue, 'she was not interested in having Mr Joyce as her pensioner; she wished to see him a free man' (*DMW* 225).

Within that freedom, whenever family worries permitted, Joyce's life could be congenial enough; Nora and he often took holidays on the continent, sometimes quite extended ones; within Paris itself their daily routines were also pleasant and very regular; Louis Gillet recollects:

> Joyce was a man of habit: 'I am so dumb,' he used to say, 'that in ten years I have not discovered another restaurant.' However, when he migrated later on to the Rue Galilée, he took his station at Fouquet's. . . . He always occupied the same table, and at the table, the same seat. The menu was also determined once and for all: marenne oysters, chicken, flap mushrooms or asparagus, cup of fruit or ice-cream. He himself did not touch anything, smoked or ordered the same muscatel, emptying three or four carafes of it nervously until half past eleven or twelve, at which time his night's work was to begin. . . .
>
> . . . He used to get up late, around eleven o'clock (having stayed up long into the night), worked after lunch and allowed himself, before his nocturnal session, a respite at the end of the afternoon. During this time of relaxation, he liked to talk, confided readily. Then he would pull himself together, get up, seize his cane (the white cane of the blind), and on my arm make his way towards the Rue Las-Cases, to the house of his friend Paul Léon, who used to take care of his affairs.
>
> [*PAE* 182–3]

Concern about his family, however, often made that routine impossible or painful. One crisis occurred when, in November 1926, his sister Eileen's husband, Frantisek Schaurek, committed suicide in Trieste, after it was discovered that he had embezzled funds. Eileen, meanwhile, was on a trip to Dublin, and wired that she would visit her brother and Nora in Paris – entirely unaware of what her husband had done. Joyce could not face telling her when she arrived, or even telling Nora, so for several days he kept the horrible news to himself during the visit by Eileen. As he later told Weaver:

> . . . my brother-in-law in Trieste blew his brains out while my sister was on her way from Ireland to Trieste. He was dead when she [Eileen] was here and neither she nor my wife . . . knew about it. . . . I had a dreadful time playing up to them and was almost in the 'jimjams' for about a month after. He lived, unconscious, for 26 hours after rolling his eyes from side to side.
>
> [*SL* 320]

In his agitation, Joyce left it – cruelly – for Stanislaus to reveal the news to Eileen upon her arrival in Trieste; she refused to believe it and demanded that the coffin be dug up and opened. Meanwhile, Stanislaus had told the children their father had died in a car accident; Bozena (Beatrice) did not discover the truth until she found a newspaper clipping among her mother's things while looking for a handkerchief (Delimata 49–50). Together, Joyce and Stanislaus took on the financial burden of contributing to the support of Eileen and the children (*N* 311); for Stanislaus, that meant a postponement of his planned marriage, which took place in August 1928, to Nelly Lichtensteiger, when he was forty-three years old.

We have seen the importance to Joyce of friendship, but that importance paled next to the supremacy for him of family. Thomas McGreevy recalled a remark Joyce made: "'I love my wife and my daughter and my son", he once said to me half-dreamily. "For the rest of the world – ." He held up his hands' (in Dawson 307). As early as 1903, before he had even met Nora and years before they had any children of their own, he wrote to his mother that 'no-one that has raised up a family has failed utterly in my opinion' (*LII* 39), and Sylvia Beach reports that in later years 'Joyce, with his patriarchal ideas, regretted that he hadn't ten children' (Beach 43) – that is, as many as his own father had.

That father died in December 1931. Joyce was grief-stricken: McGreevy records his friend suddenly breaking down on a Paris street and crying for several minutes before he could regain his composure (in Dawson 315). John Joyce had remained loving and loyal to his oldest son, whom he had not seen in decades; his granddaughter, Eileen's daughter, remembers that 'whenever we visited "Pappie" through the years, we took him a bottle of John Jameson, his favorite whiskey, and we invariably found him reading up on Uncle Jim' (Delimata 50). Others paint a sad picture of a man broken by the loss of discipline that had been provided by his wife; according to Constantine Curran:

Deprived by her gentle restraint, demoralization set in and his family, powerless to help, gradually scattered. Presently there was complete collapse, and the old man suffered ignominy before he was at length rescued by friends like Alf Bergan and the Medcalfes, generous, understanding, and forbearing good Samaritans, who took him into their care for his last twelve years or more.

[Curran 70]

His son felt 'self-accusation' at his father's death; he wrote to T. S. Eliot that his father 'had an intense love for me and it adds anew to my grief and remorse that I did not go to Dublin to see him for so many years. I kept him constantly under the illusion that I would come and was always in correspondence with him but an instinct which I believed in held me back from going, much as I longed to.' To Weaver he testified that 'I got from him his portraits, a waistcoat, a good tenor voice, and an extravagant licentious disposition (out of which, however, the greater part of any talent I may have springs)' (*LI* 311–12).

Grief at his father's death was complicated by concern in regard to his own children. Their welfare had not been fostered by the nomadic lives they had lived – changing their abodes and their schools from Trieste to Zurich, back to Trieste and then to Paris, while within each city as well there were frequent moves: during their years in Paris the Joyces had – according to one perhaps conservative count – seventeen addresses (*DMW* 173)! Even Joyce's own many moves as a child and adolescent from one neighbourhood of Dublin to another had been less hectic and wrenching than the moves experienced by his children. Inevitably, such dislocations played havoc with their education; in later years Lucia remembered a time when she and Giorgio had to be dragged – one child in each of Joyce's hands – by force to school (*DMW* 222). Back in Trieste, Lucia lost a year, and the Joyces gave up on formal schooling for Giorgio – at the age of fourteen – and employed a private tutor (*JJ* 471). Their parents, especially their father, were unable to provide for the two children the discipline, clear goals and sense of purpose that might have replaced what was lost in their not having a measure of permanence in their homes and their education.

Giorgio was, no doubt inevitably, both like and unlike his father. He was apparently not particularly fond of literature; one day when a friend remarked that he had seen Giorgio reading a book, Joyce professed astonishment (*JJ* 434). But Giorgio had a beautiful voice (bass, although later – after a throat operation – baritone), of which his father was justifiably proud. He had unclear or non-existent career plans, and Joyce spoke in an unpublished letter of his fear that he saw in his son 'a state of listlessness' (*N* 234). Giorgio had thought of studying medicine, and then for a while – like his father before him – had a short, abortive career working in a bank. In time he settled on a singing career, and he seriously studied for a number of years at the Schola Cantorum; he had his professional debut in 1929, at the age of twenty-three (*JJ* 556, 611).

By then Giorgio had been having an affair for some time with Helen Kastor Fleischman, a wealthy married American Jewish woman about eleven years older than he. After her divorce in 1929, they planned to marry, much to Nora's dismay (in part arising from their differences in age); just weeks before the marriage took place, 10 December 1930, Joyce reported that Nora was 'extremely pessimistic' about it (*SL* 355), and even that she and Helen were 'not on speaking terms' (in *N* 346); but within two weeks after the wedding he was able to say that 'my wife and daughter-in-law are at present on the most affectionate terms' (*LIII* 208), and they did indeed become quite close.

It was at least in part because of Helen Joyce's feelings that after so many years Joyce and Nora decided to marry, for Helen did not want to bear a child who might in any way seem 'illegitimate' or whose right to carry the family name might be questioned, and Joyce very much hoped that Giorgio and Helen would soon provide him with a grandchild (*N* 339). He had also begun to be concerned about complications in his estate were he not married; that he was receptive in any case is indicated by the fact that somewhat earlier, in 1927, J. F. Byrne, on a trip to Paris, had with Nora's permission – even urging – raised the possibility of marriage with Joyce, 'and he assented warmly' (Byrne 149–50). His new attitude was perhaps not so surprising, after all, given that Nora and Joyce always spoke of each other as husband and wife and had for some time both taken to wearing wedding bands. Still, it was not until 1931 that – 'for testamentary reasons', as their solicitor put it – they decided to marry under English law and thereby took up residence in England for several months. Always observant of the significance of dates, Joyce chose his father's birthday, 4 July, for the marriage date. They had not wanted the occasion to be public, so they were bitterly mortified to see a headline that morning in the *Daily Mirror*, 'Author to Wed' (*N* 165, 356).

It did not take a marriage for there to be evidence that Nora was and remained the most important person in Joyce's life. As early as 1908 he had written to her that 'our children (much as I love them) *must not* come between us' (*LII* 242), and as late as 1935 he claimed to Weaver that his wife 'personally is probably worth both of her children rolled together and multiplied by three' (*LI* 367). Friends testify that he especially delighted in her wit; an example Mary Colum gives is Nora's description of someone's run-down flat as 'not fit to wash a rat in' (Colum 77). Acquaintances who under-estimated Nora or her closeness to her husband soon discovered that, if they attempted to invite him to social functions without her, he would simply refuse.[11] More dramatically, when she was hos-pitalised for treatment of suspected cancer in November 1928, Joyce insisted on having an extra bed put in her room so he could stay there too; when she eventually underwent a hysterectomy in Febru-ary 1929, he again slept by her hospital bedside, this time for several weeks (*JJ* 607). There were, however, points of friction, which occa-sionally led Nora to threaten to leave him – often because of his drinking bouts. Stuart Gilbert's diary records his presence one evening when Nora informed him 'she won't live with him any more'; Joyce, dejected, said that he 'must have her'; Nora seemed adamant as Gilbert left, but when he rang them up a short while later, 'Mrs J. answers, says she's "given in again". So that's that' ('Selections' 24–5).

But Joyce could also be troubled by Nora; notably, she showed relatively little interest in his art and even professed indifference to or ignorance of *Ulysses*; shortly after its publication he wrote to her begging, 'O my dearest, if you would only turn to me even now and read that terrible book which has now broken the heart in my breast'; two years later he cut the pages of an edition with a list of mistakes at the end, still hoping she would read it (*LIII* 63, 86). For her part she remarked once to Maria Jolas, 'You can't imagine what it means for a woman like me to be Mrs. James Joyce', and on another occasion, 'I don't know whether he is a genius or not, but I do know he is absolutely unique'.[12]

In February 1932 Helen gave birth to a son, Stephen James Joyce, an event which moved Joyce to pair the birth with his own father's death a couple of months earlier, in a poem, 'Ecce Puer':

Of the dark past
A child is born;
With joy and grief
My heart is torn.

Calm in his cradle
The living lies.
May love and mercy
Unclose his eyes!

Young life is breathed
On the glass;
The world that was not
Comes to pass.

A child is sleeping:
An old man gone.
O, father forsaken,
Forgive your son!

[*Portable Joyce* 663]

Despite her Jewish background, Helen wanted to have the baby baptised, an idea of which Joyce would not have approved; so the baptism was performed secretly, with the Colums acting as godparents. Yet years later, when Mary Colum accidentally revealed what had happened, Joyce seemed unconcerned (Colum 132–3).

He and Nora were both greatly disturbed when in 1934 Giorgio and Helen decided, in part to further his career, to travel to the United States (*JJ* 672–3). While there Giorgio's professional life did get an encouraging boost from the famous Irish singer John McCormack, and he gave a couple of radio concerts; but problems arose as a result of the expectations of audiences (especially Irish–Americans) that – the son, after all, of the famous Irish novelist James Joyce – he would be a stereotypical Irish tenor 'and croon to them about *Mother Machree* and *A Little Bit of Heaven*' (*LI* 366).

Giorgio and Helen returned to Europe; they made another trip to the States at the end of 1937 and early 1938 (*SL* 389). By then there were some strains in their marriage, and Helen was becoming increasingly prone to nervous breakdowns; by 1939 they were no longer living together (*JJ* 728). Moreover Giorgio, who had once greatly disapproved of his father's drinking, had begun to drink heavily, and not the wine to which his father was accustomed, but whiskey and cognac; by the 1940s he struck at least one sympathetic visitor, the Joyce scholar and collector John J. Slocum, as 'a tragic dipsomaniac' (*N* 258, 332, 471). This was an unexpected turn, perhaps, given his father's remark, once – presumably when he was deeply troubled about Giorgio's sister – that 'Jane Austen named my children': 'Sense and Sensibility' (Colum 151).

The deep devotion between Joyce and Nora was often disturbing to their daughter, who was also made to realise by the marriage plans that they had never been married before; during a family argument between Lucia and Nora, her mother called her a 'bastard', and Lucia shouted, 'And who made me one?' (*DMW* 449). Lucia had been deeply disturbed by Giorgio's marriage as well, for she and her brother had been very close, and she felt she was losing him (*N* 350). There was in fact much that troubled Lucia, and in dealing with her pain and its effects on Joyce we must confront the saddest episodes and aspects of his life: as he wrote to Weaver, 'Perhaps I shall survive and perhaps the raving madness I write will survive and perhaps it is very funny. One thing is sure, however. *Je suis bien triste*' (*LI* 362).

We have at least some record, especially in his letters and the memoirs of his friends, of Joyce's agony over his daughter's illness; we must largely attempt to imagine her own suffering. Lucia seems to have been even more affected than Giorgio by all their changes of homes, schools and even languages – as she had to learn German in Zurich, then French in Paris as an adolescent, while the family spoke both English and Italian at home. By the time of their arrival in Paris in 1920 Joyce was already concerned about her: 'I do not know what to do about my daughter', he acknowledged to John Quinn in an unpublished letter (*JJ* 485). In late adolescence she developed a serious interest in becoming a dancer and studied in a succession of dancing schools, working six hours a day; between 1926 and 1929 she appeared in a number of recitals in Paris and once in Brussels (*JJ* 612). At her last performance, in May 1929, she did not receive the prize her father – and, according to his account, the audience – felt she deserved: 'Lucia's disqualification for the dancing prize was received by a strong protest from a good half of the audience (*not* friends of ours) who called out repeatedly "Nous réclamons l'irlandaise! Un peu de justice, messieurs!" She got the best notice, I think' (*LI* 280). Nevertheless it was decided that her career as a dancer must end, probably because she lacked 'the physical stamina'.[13]

Lucia had other talents as well, and she began to pursue her abilities in drawing. She was quite skilful, as anyone who has seen her intricate 'lettrines' – or ornamented initial letters – can attest; their intricacy suggests both the *Book of Kells* and the palimpsest of Joyce's own *Finnegans Wake*, a connection he made in a letter to Lucia: 'Lord knows what my prose means. In a word, it is pleasing to the ear. And your drawings are pleasing to the eye. That is enough, it seems to me' (*LI* 341). Still, she lost interest in the possibility of that career too, so that in 1931 – in a still unpublished passage in a letter to Weaver – Joyce wrote:

> She having given up dancing began to attend drawing classes and seems to have astonished her master by her designs, then she gave that up and she began to write a novel. Lately she seems to be attending dress shows, she is full of energy to do something but I do not know how to direct it.
>
> [In Scott 80]

He did not lose all hope or interest in her drawing, however, and as late as 1936 – by which time her mental illness had become extremely serious – he arranged (without her knowing it was at his expense) for the publication of her initial letters in *A Chaucer ABC*, which appeared in July 1936 with a preface by Louis Gillet. A month earlier Joyce had expressed his rationale to Weaver – in a letter in which he speaks of his daughter as being 'in a madhouse' – by saying that his 'idea is not to persuade her that she is a Cézanne but that on her 29th birthday . . . she may see something to persuade her that her whole past has not been a failure' (*SL* 380).

Lucia's illness first became acute and undeniable in 1932: on 2 February, Joyce's fiftieth birthday, she became violent and threw a chair at Nora; Giorgio had to take her to a nursing or mental home, where she remained for a few days, being released only a week or so before the birth of Helen and Giorgio's baby boy. In April she expressed an interest in going to England, and her parents planned the trip, but at the railroad station in Paris she had a screaming fit and made it impossible to go; attempts to comfort and appease her led her to stay with the Léons for a bit over a week; she then said she wanted to stay instead with the Colums (*JJ* 645; 650). Mary Colum was fond of Lucia and, although she herself was not in good health, agreed to the visit. It was not an easy time, and Colum, afraid that Lucia might harm or kill herself, slept in the same bed with her and pinned Lucia's nightdress to her own. Joyce arranged for a psychiatrist to visit each day on the pretence that he was treating Mary Colum, and the two women would sit with him each day and talk, the older one 'posing as the patient' while the psychiatrist asked them both questions (Colum 138–9).

The next month Lucia was tricked into entering a clinic, where she stayed for several weeks; while she was there a physician diagnosed her (with how much accuracy it is impossible for us to tell) as schizophrenic, specifically as hebephrenic (*JJ* 651). (Hebephrenia, a form of schizophrenia, is defined as a psychosis characterised 'by disorganized thinking, shallow and inappropriate affect, unpredictable giggling, silly and regressive behavior and mannerisms, and frequent hypochondriacal complaints. Delusions and hallucinations, if present, are transient and not well organized.'[14])

As the seriousness of Lucia's condition became more and more evident, Joyce's reactions were inevitably tortured and complex. Among the foremost of his responses was a sense of guilt and self-accusation; he recognised the problems brought about by the unsettled life his daughter had always led, but he also blamed his own character, even – according to Gillet – 'the abnormality that his genius possessed', a thought that 'crucified him': 'It was his fault; he was the father.'[15] In 1933 Paul Léon wrote to Weaver on his own, expressing his concern that every time he met Joyce 'some new origin of her condition has been discovered'; the one invariable seemed to be 'the fact that he is the culprit' (*LIII* 287). In context, it is not clear if the accusation comes from Joyce or from others – or both. Certainly some people besides himself blamed him, however much they might hide that feeling – although a few, like Stanislaus Joyce, may not in fact have been silent on that score (*DMW* 316).

It is not surprising that one major reaction on Joyce's part was denial, the claim that – as he wrote Weaver in 1934 – his daughter was not mad but that 'the poor child is just a poor girl who tried to do too much, to understand too much' (*LI* 346). Ironically though understandably, when Helen Joyce later suffered a breakdown that turned out to be less serious than Lucia's condition, and curable, Joyce was able to use terms in regard to his daughter-in-law that he could never apply to his daughter: 'complètement folle' ('completely mad'), 'la plupart du temps en plein délire' ('out of her mind most of the time') (*SL* 403).

Above all, as he saw his daughter's suffering Joyce himself underwent profound depression – a state he himself described as one in which he had 'nothing in my heart but rage and despair, a blind man's rage and despair' (*LI* 367). He became obsessed with her condition and his attempts to help her, leaving aside for prolonged periods even his art and his work on *Finnegans Wake*.

Lucia was no less attached to him; she wrote to him in October 1934, 'Father, if ever I take a fancy to anybody I swear to you on the head of Jesus that it will not be because I am not fond of you.'[16] In fact, by then she was quite experienced sexually; according to Brenda Maddox, 'as she gradually lost control of herself, Lucia became promiscuous and was taken advantage of'.[17] Sometimes she was very forward; her cousin Bozena, Eileen's daughter, reports that on a visit Lucia paid to the family in Ireland 'we were embarrassed by the fact that when we went on a jaunting cart, as Lucia preferred, she never wore underclothes. Picnics were a failure because the boys I knew didn't care for her whims' – among them one in which 'she would sit on their laps and try to undo their trousers'.[18] She was pretty, by all reports, despite the cast in her eye that sometimes made it seem as if she were squinting; as Mary Colum put it, 'the odd way her eyes were set was noticeable, but did not prevent her from being attractive-looking' (Colum 76). In 1930 she underwent an operation to correct that condition; it took twenty minutes, and although its outcome seems to have been uncertain, Joyce was satisfied with the result (*SL* 347).

Lucia very much wanted to marry, and in the French custom the Joyces provided a *dot*, or dowry, for her. But she felt frustrated by her sense that 'the young men who came to the house talked more to her father than they did to her' (Colum 136). One of her crushes was on Samuel Beckett, who in addition to idolising her father had also come to be quite close to her brother Giorgio. But he did not share Lucia's love interest, and his feelings for Joyce as for a father-figure made him feel awkward about advances from Joyce's daughter. The Joyces, however, were not averse to a relationship between Lucia and Beckett, so when he finally got up the courage to tell her that he was not romantically interested in her and only came to the flat to see her father, her parents – especially Nora, who felt that Beckett had merely led Lucia on – were furious and informed him that he was no longer welcome in their home, in a break that agonised the young man (Bair 100–1). Joyce and Beckett were eventually reconciled, so much so that in January 1938, when Beckett – walking along a Paris street, having left a café late one night – was stabbed in the chest by a pimp whom he had refused money, Joyce was one of the first people to visit him in the hospital and then insisted that

Beckett be given a private room at Joyce's expense (Bair 278). In later years, Beckett remained one of Lucia's most constant friends, regularly corresponding with her during her final institutionalisation.

Among others in whom Lucia was at one time or another more or less seriously interested were Robert McAlmon and the sculptor Alexander Calder, about whom there is a touching passage in an 'Autobiography' she wrote in later years:

> Sandy Calder was an american also he was a jew I think he had curly hair and was sort of an artist. he had a strange kind of circus which he invented himself. We were in love but I think he went away. Anyway he never wrote to me and I don't know what became of him.
>
> [Hayman 201]

(In the same document she wrote: 'Then I knew Samuel Beckett who was half Jewish he became my boy friend and he was very much in love with me but I could not marry him as he was too tall for me' [202].)

Another Jew with whom she became involved was Paul Léon's brother-in-law (Lucie's brother), Alexander Ponisovsky, through whom in fact the Léons had first met the Joyces; apparently it was because of pressure from Léon that Ponisovsky actually proposed to Lucia in May 1932. The proposal was accepted, to Joyce's pleasure but to Nora and Giorgio's horror, for they recognised that Lucia was in no condition to be married. She broke off the engagement within a few days, then became re-engaged the next day – and eventually broke it off again, permanently (*N* 376, 382).

Through all the problems Lucia's condition produced, Joyce steadfastly refused to entertain the possibility that he might place her permanently in a mental institution: 'I will not do so', he wrote to Weaver, 'as long as I see a single chance of hope for her recovery, nor blame her or punish her for the great crime she has committed in being a victim to one of the most elusive diseases known to man and unknown to medicine' (*LIII* 385–6). For all his despair, he always spoke optimistically with Lucia herself and kept up an encouraging and light tone in all his letters to her, urging that she 'not give way to moments of melancholy': 'Some day or other everything will change for you', he assured her in April 1935. 'And sooner than you might believe.' In a moving letter in June of the previous year he had written, 'I see great progress in your last letter but at the same time there is a sad note which we do not like. Why do you always sit at the window? No doubt it makes a pretty picture but a girl walking in the fields also makes a pretty picture' (*LI* 365, 342).

The Joyces sought help from a series of doctors and hospitals in much of France and elsewhere as well, including England, Switzerland, and Belgium. In 1934 they went to see Carl Gustav Jung in Zurich, by whom Joyce had declined to be analysed more than a decade earlier; Joyce was not too proud to seek help for his daughter from a doctor whom he had refused to go to himself. Indeed he would try anything, and Jung was the twentieth doctor they had consulted on Lucia's case in only three years! At first Jung seemed to have some success with Lucia, but he finally decided that hers was an exceptional case not amenable to psychoanalytic treatment; Jung, who knew Joyce's work and had written an essay on it, later told Richard Ellmann that Lucia and her father 'were like two people going to the bottom of a river, one falling and the other diving' (*JJ* 676, 679, 681).

The costs for all this treatment were enormous, and they took up a great deal of Joyce's income. He wrote to Weaver – much of the money was hers, after all – in 1936 that 'I am blamed by everybody for sacrificing that precious metal money to such an extent for such a purpose when it could be all done so cheaply and quietly by locking her up in an economical mental prison for the rest of her life'. But, he added, 'If you have ruined yourself for me as seems highly probable why will you blame me if I ruin myself for my daughter?' (*SL* 381). Weaver's help was not solely financial; in 1935, at her invitation, Lucia stayed with her in London for several sometimes harrowing weeks; all one night she slept holding on to Lucia's hand (Delimata 54). Lucia had been brought to London by Eileen, who then took her to Ireland, where her presence also created strain and difficulties. Eileen's two daughters, Bozena and Nora, had difficulty with Lucia, who ran away more than once; once she painted the living room of the bungalow in which they lived entirely black; she tried to commit suicide, and it became a daily ritual for Bozena to remove the handle of the gas taps and lock up the meter. Lucia put an advertisement in the paper, 'Wanted, Chinese lessons'; it may have been a code, and Lucia disappeared for three days. When she was found in another town, she was 'drugged'. Eventually she was taken to a home in Finglas and put into a straitjacket (Delimata 56–7), before her return first to London and Weaver's care, then to a bungalow in the country, in Surrey, but finally to St Andrew's Hospital, in Northampton. She could not be kept there against her will unless her parents committed her, and that they were unwilling to do, so she was returned to Paris. She stayed for three weeks in the home of Maria Jolas, but she finally had to be transferred – again in a straitjacket – to a mental institution in Ivry, in March 1936 (*JJ* 685–6).

Joyce's anguish over Lucia could poison his relationships with other people; despite all that she had done, he suspected that even Harriet Shaw Weaver did not have the complete sympathy for – and faith in – Lucia that she might have. He wrote to her in May 1935 with the unfair impatience of a desperate father:

> What I would like to know if you are writing to me is whether you liked Lucia or not. She said she was sending me a letter she had from you but of course, scatterbrain forgot to put it in. She may be mad, of course, as all the doctors say but I do not like you to mention her in the same breath with my cousin or sister or anybody else. If she should be so mentioned then it is I who am mad.
> [*SL* 377]

Similarly defensive of his son, in late 1939 when Léon seemed to be taking Helen's side in the split-up of Giorgio's marriage, Joyce broke off their friendship; Léon was shocked and hurt, but in this case the break was short-lived (*JJ* 728–9, 733).

Padraic Colum has written of a period in which Lucia seemed to have turned against her father; when Colum spoke of all the hardships Joyce had endured, she did mention – 'without sympathy' – that 'I saw him crying when he found he couldn't see to write' (Colum 137). During much of this time, in fact, Joyce continued to suffer from problems with his eyes; by the mid-1920s he had undergone nine operations, yet by 1928 he could no longer read print. In 1930, however, his consultation with Dr Alfred Vogt of Zurich produced something of a turnaround; in May of that year Dr Vogt performed the eleventh – and last – surgical operation on Joyce's eyes, and the results were gratifyingly successful (*JJ* 573, 603, 657). For the rest of his life Joyce continued to need constant consultation, and he sometimes had relapses – in part because his distracted worries over Lucia made him postpone trips to Zurich to see Dr Vogt – but he was never again so incapacitated as he had been.

Even within Joyce's troubles and despair, there could sometimes be 'fun at Finnegan's wake'. For Joyce, according to his friend Jacques Mercanton, 'his book was a monster. Yet, that monster was his only pleasure' (*PAE* 218). Carola Giedion-Welcker remembers how Nora used to complain during the years of her husband's composition of *Work in Progress*:

> 'I can't sleep anymore, I can't sleep anymore.' I said, 'Why?' And she said, 'Well, Jim is writing at his book.' I said, 'But what does it matter to you?' She said, 'I go to bed, and then that man sits in the next room and continues laughing about his own writing. And then I knock at the door, and I say, now Jim, stop writing or stop laughing.'
>
> [Kain, 'Interview' 96]

No one who knows *Finnegans Wake* well could be surprised at such laughter; no one who knows it even slightly will be surprised that it took a great deal of difficult work and massive efforts, over many years, to compose. So unusual and encyclopedic an achievement demanded a highly unusual and (sometimes literally) encyclopedic mode of composition; Stuart Gilbert, for example, recorded in his diary some of Joyce's methods for the section of *Work in Progress* published in 1930 as *Haveth Childers Everywhere*:

> For the 'town references', he scoured all the capital towns in the Encyclopedia and recorded in his black notebook all the 'punnable' names of streets, buildings, city-founders. Copenhagen, Budapest, Oslo, Rio I read to him. Unfortunately he made the entries in his black notebook himself and when he wanted to use them, the reader found them illegible. On the last day he inserted punnishly the names of 60 Mayors of Dublin (taken from the Dublin Postal directory of 1904).[19]

Although published in 1930, the section of *Work in Progress* of which Gilbert speaks appears toward the end of *Finnegans Wake*, for Joyce's work on his book was quite unchronological. In contrast to his basically straightforward methods of attack for both the *Portrait* and *Ulysses*, in this case Joyce would for example tackle one fragment in Book I, another in Book III, and postpone confronting sections of Book II – the section dealing extensively, as it turns out, with HCE and ALP's daughter Issy. ('What is amaid today todo? So angelland all weeping bin that Izzy most unhappy is' [*FW* 257.1–2]).

For long stretches Joyce left off work on the *Wake* altogether, but he always came back to it, quoting William Blake's aphorism (in *Proverbs of Hell*) that 'if the fool would persist in his folly he would become wise' (Mercanton, *PAE* 215). He did of course persist and came at last to the final word; Louis Gillet remembers:

> 'In *Ulysses*', he told me once, 'in order to convey the mumbling of a woman falling asleep, I wanted to finish with the faintest word that I could possibly discover. I found the word *yes*, which is barely pronounced, which implies consent, abandonment, relaxation, the end of all resistance. For "Work in Progress", I tried to find something better if possible. This time I discovered the most furtive word, the least stressed, the weakest in English, a word which is not even a word, which barely sounds between the teeth, a breath, a mere nothing, the article *the*.'
>
> [*PAE* 197]

He was willing to indicate the last word of the book before he would consent to reveal its title. He had wagered 1000 francs against his friends' guessing it (he had told only Nora what it would be), but in August 1938 he apparently dropped a few too many hints to Eugene Jolas, who guessed it would be *Finnegans Wake* (*LIII* 427); Joyce's reaction was a wistful 'Ah Jolas, you've taken something out of me' (Jolas, 'My Friend' 16).

In November 1938 Joyce was able to write his friend Paul Ruggiero, 'Hip, Hip! Ho finito quel maledetto libro' (*LI* 403) – he had finished the 'damned book'. A rush was made by his publishers – T. S. Eliot's firm, Faber and Faber – to prepare what by now must have seemed the ritual copy for Joyce's birthday, and when 2 February 1939 came he was presented with a set of page proofs as the 'book', although its actual publication had to wait until May (*SL* 394). Its reception ran the gamut from awe and adulation to utter bewilderment to cynical scepticism to vitriolic attack. A surprisingly responsive review by Oliver St John Gogarty capsulised the complex reactions of many readers; he began by granting that 'Joyce's language is more than a revolt against classicism, it is more than a return to the freedom of slang and thieves' punning talk. It is an attempt to get at words before they clarify in the mind.' Gogarty went on to recognise the 'immense erudition employed', recalling the 'superhuman knowledge' the young Joyce had demonstrated in Dublin; but he could not resist the conclusion – the accusation – that it was all in the end a 'colossal leg-pull' (in Deming 673–5).

Joyce had produced, in *Ulysses*, a book that was already widely regarded as the greatest novel of the twentieth century, and then in *Finnegans Wake* one of the most amazing and formidable works in all

of literary history. What could come next? Naturally many people
wondered. Joyce's responses were general and not always consist-
ent: he spoke of doing something perhaps 'very simple and very
short'; perhaps about the morning after ('Wait until Finnegan wakes',
he used to say to Léon); perhaps – inspired by the Greek resistance
at the start of the Second World War – about the modern Greek
revolution for independence.[20] The onset of the war in 1939 of course
affected the Joyces just as it did all Europe; it was no doubt myopic
yet a statement one could wish had been obeyed when he remarked,
'Let them leave Poland in peace and occupy themselves with
Finnegans Wake' (Mercanton, *PAE* 249).

He looked upon the developments in recent European history
with horror. At first he would try to be jocular about the idiocies of
Hitler and Mussolini, as when in 1934 he wrote to Weaver that he
was afraid that they would have 'few admirers in Europe' aside
from Wyndham Lewis and Ezra Pound (*LIII* 311); but as the terrors
of Nazism became even clearer, his old detestation of anti-semitism
– which he called 'the easiest of all prejudices to foment'[21] – and his
antipathy to all forms of authoritarianism were reinforced. In the
dark days of the late 1930s he gave concrete assistance to a number
of Jews attempting to flee from German control. Through his own
connections and energetic efforts, he was able to help Hermann
Broch, the Austrian novelist and critic whom Joyce had never met
but whose *James Joyce und die Gegenwart* (*James Joyce and the Present*)
had appeared in 1936, to escape to the United States, together with
'two other people' – and Joyce seems to have helped at least a
dozen others as well. Dominic Manganiello has aptly spoken of
these efforts as exemplifying a commitment which 'took the form of
humanitarian action so typical of Bloom. At the crucial moment,
Joyce had repaid Alfred Hunter's gesture towards him of over thirty
years before.'[22]

After a time, Joyce had to worry about his own safety and that of
his family. Paris was in imminent danger of being lost to the Nazis
when, in December 1939, Joyce, Nora and their seven-year-old grandson Stephen left the city for a small village almost two hundred miles
away, Saint-Gérand-le-Puy, where the Jolases had a home which
also housed Maria Jolas's school for French and American children;
the Joyces stayed in the village, not far from Lyon and very near
Vichy and German-occupied France, almost a year, using for their
subsistence money provided through the American Embassy for
British subjects in France.[23] For a time they lived in a flat, and for a

while with the Jolases. The fall of Paris in May 1940 led to the arrival of other refugees, including Beckett, Giorgio – a particular concern, for he was of military age – and the Léons; Joyce and Paul Léon were quickly reconciled.[24]

Unfortunately, after a time Léon returned to Paris, now under the Nazis. While there, he helped save some of the Joyce family's property – and Joyce's papers – from their flat; he had to buy some of what he rescued when an unscrupulous landlord held an illegal auction. Léon deposited the Joyce papers with the Irish Ambassador for safe keeping; soon he realised that at last he had to escape, but he wanted to wait until his son took his baccalauréat examination. On that day he was arrested by the Gestapo. He was murdered by a guard during a forced march in Silesia, probably in April 1942.[25]

Sylvia Beach was also interned, in 1942, but she was released after six months. In December 1941 a German officer had been enraged when she refused to sell him her last copy of *Finnegans Wake*; when, two weeks later, she again refused, he told her that all her goods would be confiscated, then left. Within two hours she hid her entire stock in another apartment, and the shop was completely empty; Shakespeare and Company was closed.[26]

Joyce had been attacked by severe stomach pains upon his arrival at St-Gérand; the trouble was thought to be his 'nerves', but by the latter months of 1940 his condition had worsened, although his illness was still not correctly diagnosed (*JJ* 729, 733). It came to seem imperative that the family leave France; Léon had gone back to Paris and Maria Jolas had left for the United States. Going there would have been a possibility for the Joyces as well, but they seem never to have entertained it very seriously (*N* 449). Among the many things they had to worry about was whether or not Lucia would be permitted to travel with them. In the end they chose to attempt to go where they had received refuge in the last war, Zurich. But this time it was much more difficult, and the task was not made any easier by Joyce's refusal to give up his British passport in favour of one from neutral Ireland; he felt that to do so now would be both disloyal and undignified, and Giorgio felt the same.[27] It is a terrible sign of the nature of the times that a major obstacle in gaining permission for the Joyces to enter Switzerland was the denial by the Swiss authorities on the grounds that Joyce was Jewish! That was the limit, Joyce wrote a friend: 'C'est le bouquet, vraiment' (*LIII* 492). Horribly, evidence had to be garnered that he was not a Jew. Meanwhile in Zurich itself notable citizens rallied on his behalf; they included the critic Jacques

Mercanton, the Mayor of the city, and the Rector of the university. The Swiss government then demanded a very large financial guarantee, 500 000 French francs; even when it was reduced to 300 000 the sum was more than Joyce could provide; appropriately if ironically, most of the money was deposited in Zurich for him by two Jews: Edmund Brauchbar and Siegfried Giedion (Nadel 14).

Arranging for Giorgio's permission to leave France was also difficult but was finally managed, and they decided to depart even though they were not able to bring Lucia with them out of the hospital in Pornichet, on the coast of Brittany, where she and other patients had been transferred from Ivry; Joyce and Nora hoped to arrange for her to be sent to Zurich later. The Joyces – James and Nora, and Giorgio and Stephen – left St-Gérand 14 December and arrived in Zurich on the 17th (*JJ* 738–9). They settled in as best they could.

Early the next month, on Thursday, 9 January 1941, Joyce and Nora went as they often did to the Kronenhalle Restaurant for dinner, but he ate little or nothing (*JJ* 740); that was not all that unusual in his last years, when 'he always toyed with his food as if searching for something, and would then push back his plate with a disgusted look: he could put up with almost no food. . . . After the first mouthful he would light a cigarette, he had finished his dinner. We did not suspect him to be sick' (Gillet, *PAE* 170). He had refrained from getting a thorough examination for his stomach pains, but late that night he had so severe an attack of cramps that a doctor was called; the next day an ambulance removed him to the Red Cross Hospital (the Schwesterhaus vom Roten Kreuz); left behind next to his bed were two books, a Greek dictionary and Oliver St John Gogarty's *I Follow St. Patrick* (Giedion-Welcker, *PAE* 279).

An X-ray revealed that he had a perforated ulcer. It was decided that surgery was immediately needed; Joyce thought it might be cancer and that that fact was being hidden from him, but Giorgio assured him otherwise. The operation, performed on Saturday the 11th, seemed to be a success, and on awakening Joyce confessed to Nora that he had feared 'I wouldn't get through it'. But on Sunday he weakened, and at 2:15 a.m., Monday the 13th of January 1941, he died, his superstitions about numbers and dates curiously verified. The clinical diagnosis on the postmortem report specified a 'perforated ulcer, generalized peritonitis' (*JJ* 741).

Joyce's last bit of correspondence had been addressed to Stanislaus, who had been compelled by the Italian government to move from Trieste to Florence, where he was kept in semi-detention (*MBK* xx);

Joyce wrote his brother a postcard with the names and addresses of some people who might be able to help him (*LIII* 507). Stanislaus, who had refused Joyce's offer of a copy of *Finnegans Wake* on its publication, later deeply regretted that act (*MBK* xx); he gave his son, born in 1943, the name of James. Stanislaus died on Bloomsday, 1955.

Nora's situation during the war was not much more comfortable than Stanislaus's. She had a breakdown for several weeks later in 1941 (*N* 459), and throughout the war she had very little money and had to live very simply, although she was helped by a typically generous act of Harriet Shaw Weaver, who made sure that some funds which she had been about to send to Joyce were now sent to Nora; later she disguised some gifts to Nora as publishing 'advances' (*DMW* 380, 390). Money anxieties ended for Nora in the late 1940s when genuine advances on increasing sales of Joyce's books started to come in, but she was then troubled by extremely severe arthritis, and by 1950 she could no longer walk. She developed uraemia and heart trouble and died 10 April 1951 (*N* 488–9). She had not seen her daughter since before the war.

Lucia had been returned to the clinic at Ivry, near Paris; she was transferred to St Andrew's Hospital, Northampton, shortly before her mother's death. Lucia suffered a stroke in 1982 and died 12 December of that year, at St Andrew's. Giorgio stayed very close to his mother until her death; his problems with alcoholism persisted. After his divorce from Helen, he re-married, in 1954; he died in Germany 12 June 1976. Giorgio is reported to have said he 'would have been happier and had a better life if my father had been a butcher'.[28]

Joyce's funeral took place 15 January 1941 at the Fluntern cemetery. When a Catholic priest suggested a religious service, Nora – who herself would later have a religious burial – replied, 'I couldn't do that to him' (*JJ* 742). Looking at her husband's face for the last time she burst out, 'Jim, how beautiful you are!' When she died ten years later there was no room next to his grave, but in 1966 both their remains were transferred to spots next to one another (*N* 455, 491).

An obituary notice in German appeared the day before Joyce's funeral, in the *Neue Zürcher Zeitung*,[29] dated 13 January; it bore the names of Nora, George, Lucia and Stephen Joyce, and it announced the death 'this morning at two o'clock in the Red Cross Hospital, quickly and unexpectedly', of 'our beloved husband, father and grandfather, James Joyce, in his fifty-eighth year'.

Appendix: The Joyce Family

George Joyce (early 19th c.) [JJ's paternal great-great-grandfather]

James Augustine Joyce *m.* Anne McCann [JJ's paternal great-grand-parents]

James Augustine Joyce (1827 – 1865) *m. 28 February 1848* Ellen O'Connell (daughter of John O'Connell) [JJ's paternal grand-parents] [also Alicia, Charles, and William O'Connell ('Uncle Charles') (Ellen's sister and brothers)]

John Stanislaus Joyce (4 July 1849 – 29 Dec. 1931) [JJ's father]

John Murray and [   ] Flynn [JJ's maternal grandparents] [also Mrs Callanan and Mrs Lyons, JJ's great-aunts, and Mrs Callanan's daughter, Mary Ellen]

John ('Red') Murray *m.* Lillah [   ]
Lillah
Isobel
Val
Gerald

William Murray (d. 1912) *m.* Josephine Giltrap [Aunt Josephine] (d. 1924)
Alice
Kathleen ('Katsy') (b. ca. 1889)
James
Bert
Mabel
May

Mary Jane ('May') Murray (15 May 1859 – 13 August 1903) [JJ's mother]

*John Stanislaus Joyce (4 July 1849 – 29 December 1931) m. 5 May
1880 Mary Jane ('May') Murray (15 May 1859 – 13 August 1903)
[JJ's parents]*

   10 surviving children (6 girls, 4 boys); 5 children died in infancy

      E.g., male child (1881) did not survive; also Frederick (Freddie)
      (1894); male child, ca. 1896 – 1899

   James Augusta [sic] [James Augustine Aloysius] (2 February 1882
   – 13 January 1941)

   Margaret Alice ('Poppie') (18 January 1884 – March 1964) [Admitted to Sisters of Mercy (as Sister Gertrude); emigrated to New
   Zealand (1909)]

   John Stanislaus ('Stannie') (17 December 1884 – 16 June 1955) *m.
   13 August 1928* Nelly Lichtensteiger (b. 1907) [Emigrated to London after Stanislaus's death]

      James (b. 14 February 1943)

   Charles Patrick (24 July 1886 – 18 January 1941) [Emigrated to US
   1908; returned 1911] *m. 1908* Mary [   ]; *m. second wife,
   by 1931* Annie Hearne

      George

   George Alfred (4 July 1887 – 9 March 1902)

   Eileen Isabel Mary Xavier Brigid (22 January 1889 – 27 January
   1963) [Emigrated to Trieste, January 1910; returned February 1928,
   with her two daughters] *m. 12 April 1915* Frantisek [Frank] Schaurek
   (d. November 1926 [suicide])

      Bozena (Beatrice) Berta (Bertha) ('Boschenka') (b. 9 February
      1917) *m. 1941* Tadek Delimata
         Jurek (b. June 1942)
         Kamilla (b. February 1948) [Emigrated to Canada) *m.* John
         Slazenger

Solomon

Eleonora ('Nora') (b. 1919?)

Patrick (Patrizio) (b. 31 May 1923? 1935?)

Mary Kathleen ('May') (18 January 1890 – 8 December 1966) *m.*
[   ] Monaghan

(Two daughters, one son)

Ken

Eva Mary (26 October 1891 – 25 November 1957) [Emigrated to
Trieste, October 1909; returned July 1911]

Florence Elizabeth ('Florrie') (8 November 1892 – d. late 1950s?)

Mabel Josephine Anne ('Baby') (27 November 1893 – 1911)

Patrick Healy m. Catherine Mortimer [NBJ's maternal
grandparents]
Annie (d. 1940) [NBJ's mother]

Michael (1862 – 7 November 1935) [Unmarried]

Thomas (1859 – 1926) *m. 1898* Bedelia

Thomas Barnacle (d. 1921?) m. 1881 Honoraria ('Annie') Healy (d.
1940) [NBJ's parents]

Mary [Emigrated to US] *m.* William Blackmore

Nora (21 or 22 March 1884 – 10 April 1951)

Bridget ('Delia', 'Dilly') (b. 1886) [Suffered breakdown 1925] *m.*
[   ] Hitchen

Twin Daughters (b. 1889):

Peg [Emigrated to England during World War I]
Annie (d. 1924? 1925?)

Thomas [Emigrated to England]

Kathleen (1896 – 1963) [Emigrated to England] *m. 1937* John Griffin

[One boy died in infancy]

James Joyce (2 February 1882 – 13 January 1941) eloped 8 October 1904 [m. 4 July 1931] Nora Barnacle (21 or 22 March 1884 – 10 April 1951)

Giorgio (27 July 1905 – 12 June 1976) *m. 10 December 1930; subsequently divorced* Helen Kastor Fleischman (b. 1894?) [Suffered breakdown 1938, recovered 1939; another breakdown 1939; recovered by 1946, in US; d. in US 9 January 1963; had been married to Leon Fleischman (*m. 1916; legally separated 30 November 1927; divorced 1929*); they had son, David Fleischman (b. 1919)]

Stephen James Joyce (b. 15 February 1932) *m. 15 April 1955* Solange Raytchine

[Giorgio also *m. 24 May 1954 (lived together starting 1948)* Asta Jahnke-Osterwalder (mother of son and daughter by previous marriage); moved to München; d. in Konstanz]

Lucia Anna (26 July 1907 – 12 December 1982)

[Miscarriage, 4 August 1908]

Notes

Chapter 1: As All of Dublin: The Years of Youth, 1882–1904

1. Joyce, *Workshop of Daedalus*, p. 12.
2. Connolly, 'Home Is Where the Art Is'.
3. For a genealogical listing of the members of Joyce's family, see the Appendix.
4. Stanislaus Joyce, *Diary*, pp. 23, 135.
5. *Workshop*, p. 29; cf. the similar scene in regard to Isabel in *Stephen Hero*, where it ends chapter XXII (pp. 162–3). As Richard Ellmann notes, 'George died of peritonitis on March 9, 1902, as James himself was to die' (*JJ* 94).
6. 'Gas from a Burner', in *Portable Joyce*, p. 660.
7. See Bradley, pp. 69, 75, and O Clérigh, p. 196.
8. William G. Fallon, in O'Connor, pp. 43–4. Eventually the rector came to believe that 'it was a mistake to educate a boy here when his background was so much at variance with the standards of the school' (quoted in *N*, p. 51).
9. See *P*, pp. 79–81; slightly varying accounts of the bullying incident appear in *JJ*, pp. 39–40, and in Fallon, in O'Connor, pp. 46–7.
10. See Thrane, 'Joyce's Sermon on Hell'.
11. *Workshop*, p. 21; cf. *SH*, pp. 45–6.
12. *MBK*, p. 146; cf. *P*, p. 249.
13. Gorman, p. 108; in *Ulysses* the telegram has a typo: 'Nother dying come home father' (35 [3.199]).
14. Eileen Schaurek, quoted in Cixous, p. 30.
15. *MBK*, p. 233. In *Ulysses* the humane Leopold Bloom watches Simon Dedalus about a year after Mrs Dedalus's death: 'Wore out his wife: now sings. But hard to tell. Only the two themselves' (225 [11.696–701]).
16. *LI*, p. 54; cf. Bloom's plan in *Ulysses* for 'the Tweedy-Flower grand opera company', with its 'concert tour of summer music embracing the most prominent pleasure resorts, Margate with mixed bathing and firstrate hydros and spas . . .' (p. 512 [16.518–20]).
17. *JJ*, p. 168; Ellmann quotes Holloway on Joyce's 'light tenor voice' and the report in the *Freeman's Journal* on his 'sweet tenor voice'.
18. Quoted in Manganiello, p. 131.
19. Hyman, pp. 148–9; cf. *Ulysses*, p. 136 (8.553). Sinclair loaned Joyce money to finance his elopement with Nora Barnacle.
20. *Many Lines*, pp. 14, 16; cf. *It Isn't*, pp. 85–6.
21. In an odd untruth, Gogarty says 'we lived there for two years' (*It Isn't*, p. 87).
22. Quoted from an RTE film interview, in Scott, p. 103.
23. Colum, p. 88. In youth his comments were even more offensive: 'Jim

says he has an instinct for women. He scarcely ever talks decently of them, even of those he likes. He talks of them as warm, soft-skinned animals. "That one'd give you a great push." "She's very warm between the thighs, I fancy." "She has great action, I'm sure"' (Stanislaus Joyce, *Diary*, p. 15).

24. Dillon, p. 39. Brenda Maddox believes that another suitor, Michael Feeney, may have been an even closer model for Furey than Bodkin (*N*, pp. 25, 27).

Chapter 2: Standing by the Door: The Early Work

1. *Portable Joyce*, p. 658.
2. *Workshop*, p. 27.
3. This is not the paper that Stephen writes in *Stephen Hero* under that title.
4. For a fuller discussion of how epiphany may be defined, see my *Epiphany in the Modern Novel*, especially pp. 13–18, 72–81.
5. Epiphany #1, *Workshop*, p. 11; cf. *Portrait*, p. 8.
6. Epiphany #30, *Workshop*, p. 40; cf. *Portrait*, p. 252.
7. Letter to Valéry Larbaud, in Furbank, p. 121.
8. Parandowski, *PAE*, p. 159. Cf. Joyce's comment to Frank Budgen: 'I want . . . to give a picture of Dublin so complete that if the city one day suddenly disappeared from the earth it could be reconstructed out of my book' (*Making of Ulysses*, pp. 67–8).
9. 'When Yeats died on January 28, 1939, Joyce was much moved. He sent a wreath to the funeral, and conceded to a friend that Yeats was a greater writer than he, a tribute he paid to no other contemporary' (*JJ*, p. 660).
10. Cf. Yeats's 'To Ireland in the Coming Times': '*Know, that I would accounted be/ True brother of a company/ That sang, to sweeten Ireland's wrong . . .*' (*Collected Poems*, p. 49).
11. 'The Holy Office', in *Portable Joyce*, pp. 657, 659.
12. For a discussion of the possible legal repercussions for Roberts, see Atherton, pp. 29–30.
13. *LII*, pp. 291–3. The letter was published in full in *Sinn Féin* in September 1911; part of it (with the passages about Edward VII left out) had appeared in August in the Belfast *Northern Whig*.
14. These reviews are reprinted in Beja, *Dubliners and Portrait*, pp. 60, 63.

Chapter 3: The Curve of an Emotion: The Years of the *Portrait*, 1904–1914

1. *Workshop*, p. 60.
2. Curran, p. 100.
3. Svevo, n.p. [p. 4].
4. Gorman, p. 267; on the origin of the footnote, see *PAE*, p. 4.
5. *LII*, p. 100; Vincent Cosgrave nastily expanded the telegram to include the words 'Mother and bastard doing well' (*JJ*, p. 204).

6. Franco Onorati, in Melchiori, pp. 24–8; see the *James Joyce Archive: Notes, Criticism, Translations*, vol. 2, pp. 474–617.
7. For a discussion of the possible degree of truth in Cosgrave's story, see N, p. 128.
8. For Wells's review of *Portrait*, see Deming, p. 86; for Joyce's comment, see Budgen, *Myselves*, p. 189.
9. *JJ*, pp. 384–5; Delimata, p. 45.
10. When Ezra Pound wrote to the American lawyer John Quinn to make sure Huebsch was 'a reputable publisher', Quinn replied, 'Huebsch is all right if he takes Joyce's book. He is a Jew but a fairly decent Jew' (Reid 250).
11. For the *Freeman's Journal* and Boyd, see Deming, pp. 99, 302; for the *Irish Book Lover*, see Beja, *Dubliners and Portrait*, p. 80.

Chapter 4: A Touch of the Artist: The Years of *Ulysses*, 1914–1922

1. Beach, p. 40; Stanislaus Joyce, unpublished portion of diary (1907), quoted in *JJ*, p. 265; *Ulysses*, p. 193 (10.581–3).
2. Byrne, pp. 154, 157; *Ulysses*, p. 546 (17.86–7, 91).
3. Unpublished portion of diary, quoted in *JJ*, p. 265.
4. Gorman, p. 45; *MBK*, p. 43; Gillet, in *PAE*, p. 168; cf. *LI*, p. 146.
5. Budgen, *Making*, p. 105; the writer of the letter, incidentally, was Ezra Pound (*LI*, p. 126).
6. *JJ*, p. 230; Hyman, p. 170. Hyman also mentions that a Leopold Hunter received his B.A. from Trinity in 1904.
7. *JJ*, pp. 161–2; cf. Melchiori, pp. 38–9.
8. See Hélène Cixous, 'The Laugh of the Medusa'.
9. *LII*, pp. 302–3; for examples of Molly–ish prose in letters from Joyce's mother and Aunt Josephine, see *LII*, pp. 52, 138–9.
10. Stoppard, *Travesties*, p. 65. The riposte is partially anticipated by Budgen, in *Making*, p. 191.
11. *Making*, p. 284; cf. a 1904 letter to Nora: 'Can you not see the simplicity which is at the back of all my disguises?' (*LII* 49).
12. Scott, pp. 96, 221; Jane Lidderdale and Mary Nicholson end their biography of Weaver with a quotation from Samuel Beckett: 'I . . . shall think of her when I think of goodness' (*DMW*, p. 455).
13. Cixous, p. 33; *DMW*, p. 301.
14. *SL*, p. 215, and *JJ*, p. 543; in *Ulysses* Stephen remembers his pandying at Clongowes and its connection with his eyes and his failing sight, and mutters, 'Must see a dentist' (459 [15.3721]).
15. Straumann, 'Four Letters to Martha Fleischmann', in *LII*, p. 428; according to Budgen, however, Joyce's first glimpse of her was through his back garden to her window, as she pulled the toilet chain (*Myselves*, pp, 188, 191).
16. *LII*, p. 432; Straumann, p. 431; *Ulysses*, p. 229 (11.860).
17. *Myselves*, p. 188; cf. August Suter, p. 64.
18. N, pp. 205, 221, 361; cf. Maria Jolas, 'The Joyce I Knew . . .', p. 82: 'It is

my opinion that at a much earlier age than most men, Joyce left erotic preoccupations . . . behind him.' In the 1930s, when Budgen reminded him of how he used to praise women's bodies as 'desirable and provoking', Joyce replied, 'Perhaps I did. But now I don't care a damn about their bodies. I am only interested in their ·clothes' (*Making*, p. 319).

19. Maria Jolas specifies 7:00 p.m. (in Kain, 'Interview', p. 101), while Sylvia Beach gives the time as 8:00 (Fitch, p. 63).

20. *LII*, pp. 467–8. Ellmann asserts there were only eight others (*JJ*, p. 477), but there were the four Joyces, the four Schaureks (Joyce's sister Eileen, her husband, and their two daughters), Stanislaus, and two servants, for a total of eleven (Delimata, p. 47).

21. Leonard Woolf, *Beginning Again*, p. 246; Virginia Woolf, *Diary*, vol. 1, p. 140.

22. Leonard Woolf, *Beginning Again*, p. 247; Virginia Woolf, *Letters*, vol. 2, p. 242.

23. The publisher Leslie Katz, quoted in Fitch, p. 53.

Chapter 5: Work in Progress: The Years of *Finnegans Wake*, 1922–1941

1. Joyce's apparently studied response, delivered after a few months to her husband Padraic, was that 'it may be outside literature now, but its future is inside literature' (Colum, pp. 86–7).

2. Weaver repeated the formulation 'I daresay I am wrong' in reporting her misgivings in a letter to Sylvia Beach in November of the same year (*DMW* 269, 275–6).

3. *JJ* p. 593; *LI*, p. 282; Reid, p. 309.

4. This account combines both Beach, pp. 204–5, and Fitch, pp. 322–3.

5. The decision is reprinted in Gorman, pp. 317–22, and in many Random House editions of the novel, including the 1961 edition.

6. See Moscato, pp. 321, 360, and Ellmann's introduction to that volume, p. xxii.

7. Gilbert, 'Selections', p. 11; Harold Nicolson, *Diaries and Letters: 1930–1964*. Ed. Stanley Olson. (London: Collins, 1980), quoted in Epstein, p. 31.

8. Noel, p. 8. Cf. Maria Jolas: 'he was not Joyce's secretary, but a devoted friend' (Kain, 'Interview', p. 106).

9. *N*, p. 295. Nino Frank reports that, as an editor, he was once excited at hearing that D. H. Lawrence was in Paris and wondered about asking him for a contribution; Joyce's opinion was, 'That man writes really too poorly . . . Ask his friend Aldous Huxley for something instead; at least he dresses decently' (*PAE*, p. 87).

10. For estimates, see *N*, p. 296.

11. See, for example, Maria Jolas's testimony in Kain, 'Interview', p. 101.

12. In Dillon, p. 40, and in Kain, 'Interview', p. 112.

13. Ellmann's term, *JJ*, p. 612; he states that the decision was hers, with Joyce's approval; Maddox reports that at least one friend of Joyce and

Nora's believed that they made the decision and put a stop to their daughter's dancing (*N*, pp. 330–1).

14. Committee on Nomenclature and Statistics of the American Psychiatric Association, *Diagnostic and Statistical Manual of Mental Disorders*. Washington, DC: American Psychiatric Association, 1968, p. 33.
15. Gillet, *PAE*, p. 192. In a note to this passage in *Portraits of the Artist in Exile*, Willard Potts quotes Bloom, in *Ulysses*: 'If it's healthy it's from the mother. If not from the man' (p. 79 [6.329]).
16. Unpublished letter in Italian; translated by Joyce and quoted in *JJ*, p. 676.
17. Ellmann only mentions that an affair with Albert Hubbell in 1930 provided her first 'sexual involvement' (*JJ*, pp. 612–13), but Maddox convincingly shows that there were many other affairs as well (*N*, p. 333).
18. Delimata, pp. 55–6, and quoted in *N*, p. 411.
19. Gilbert, 'Selections', p. 19; see *FW*, pp. 532–54.
20. See *JJ*, p. 731; Léon, p. 291; Giedion-Welcker in Kain, 'Interview', p. 97.
21. Quoted by Maria Jolas, in Beja, 'Political Perspectives on Joyce's Work', p. 115.
22. Manganiello, p. 231; see *LIII*, p. 424, Colum, p. 149, Budgen, 'James Joyce', p. 23, and Nadel, pp. 232–5.
23. *JJ*, p. 729; *N*, pp. 447, 450.
24. *SL*, p. 401; *JJ*, p. 733.
25. *JJ*, p. 734; *N*, p. 449; Noel, p. 49. Léon's brother-in-law Alex, Lucia's former fiancé, was arrested in April 1944 and presumably died in a concentration camp (Colum, p. 136).
26. Beach, pp. 215–16; Fitch, p. 406.
27. Noel, p. 34; Mercanton, *PAE*, pp. 250–1.
28. Quoted by Maria Jolas, in Kain, 'Interview', p. 114.
29. Reproduced in Faerber and Luchsinger, *Joyce in Zürich*, p. 145; my translation.

Works Cited and Selected Bibliography

Anderson, Chester G., *James Joyce and His World* (London: Thames and Hudson, 1967).

Anderson, Margaret C., *My Thirty Years' War* (New York: Horizon, 1969).

Atherton, James, 'The Joyce of *Dubliners*', in Staley, *James Joyce Today*, pp. 28–53.

Aubert, Jacques, and Maria Jolas, eds, *Joyce & Paris: 1902 . . . 1920–1940 . . . 1975, Papers from the Fifth International James Joyce Symposium*, two vols (Paris: Éditions du C.N.R.S., 1979).

Bair, Deirdre, *Samuel Beckett: A Biography* (New York: Harcourt Brace Jovanovich, 1978).

Bauerle, Ruth, ed., *The James Joyce Songbook* (New York: Garland, 1982).

Beach, Sylvia, *Shakespeare and Company* (New York: Harcourt Brace, 1959).

Beckett, Samuel, et al., *Our Exagmination Round His Factification for Incamination of Work in Progress* (Paris: Shakespeare and Company, 1929).

_____ , *Three Plays: Ohio Impromptu, Catastrophe, and What Where* (New York: Grove, 1984).

Beja, Morris, *Epiphany in the Modern Novel* (Seattle: University of Washington Press, 1971).

_____ , *Joyce, the Artist Manqué, and Indeterminacy* (London: Colin Smythe, 1989).

_____ , 'Political Perspectives on Joyce's Work', in Aubert and Jolas, pp. 101–23.

_____ , ed., *James Joyce: Dubliners and A Portrait of the Artist as a Young Man: A Selection of Critical Essays* (London: Macmillan, 1973).

_____ , and Shari Benstock, eds, *Coping with Joyce: Essays from the Copenhagen Symposium* (Columbus: Ohio State University Press, 1989).

_____ , et al., eds, *James Joyce: The Centennial Symposium* (Urbana: University of Illinois Press, 1986).

Benstock, Bernard, *James Joyce* (New York: Frederick Ungar, 1985).

Benstock, Shari, *Women of the Left Bank: Paris, 1900–1940* (Austin: University of Texas Press, 1986).

Bowen, Zack, and James F. Carens, eds, *A Companion to Joyce Studies* (Westport: Greenwood, 1984).

Bradley, Bruce, S.J., *James Joyce's Schooldays* (Dublin: Gill and Macmillan, 1982).

Brown, Malcolm, *The Politics of Irish Literature: From Thomas Davis to W. B. Yeats* (Seattle: University of Washington Press, 1972).

Budgen, Frank, 'James Joyce', in Givens, pp. 19–26.

_____ , *James Joyce and the Making of Ulysses* (Bloomington: Indiana University Press, 1960).

_____ , *Myselves When Young* (New York: Oxford University Press, 1970).

Byrne, J. F., *Silent Years: An Autobiography with Memoirs of James Joyce and Our Ireland* (New York: Farrar, Strauss and Young, 1953).

Cerf, Bennett, *At Random: The Reminiscences of Bennett Cerf* (New York: Random House, 1977).

Cixous, Hélène, *The Exile of James Joyce*, trans. Sally A. J. Purcell (New York: David Lewis, 1972).

_____, 'The Laugh of the Medusa', trans. Keith Cohen and Paula Cohen, in Elain Marks and Isabelle De Courtivron, eds, *New French Feminisms* (New York: Schocken, 1981).

Cohn, Ruby, *Back to Beckett* (Princeton University Press, 1973).

Colum, Mary and Padraic Colum, *Our Friend James Joyce* (Garden City: Doubleday, 1958).

Connolly, Thomas E., 'Home Is Where the Art Is: The Joyce Family Gallery', *James Joyce Quarterly* 20 (Fall 1982) 11–31.

Curran, C. P., *James Joyce Remembered* (New York: Oxford University Press, 1968).

Daniel, Clifton, ed., *Chronicle of the 20th Century* (Mount Kisco: Chronicle, 1987).

Dawson, Hugh J., 'Thomas MacGreevy and Joyce', *James Joyce Quarterly* 25 (Spring 1988) 305–21.

Delimata, Bozena Berta, 'Reminiscences of a Joyce Niece', ed. Virginia Moseley, *James Joyce Quarterly* 19 (Fall 1981) 45–62.

Deming, Robert H., ed., *James Joyce: The Critical Heritage*, two vols (London: Routledge and Kegan Paul, 1970).

Dillon, Eilis, 'The Innocent Muse: An Interview with Maria Jolas', *James Joyce Quarterly* 20 (Fall 1982) 33–66.

Dujardin, Édouard, *Le Monologue intérieur, son apparition, ses origines, sa place dans l'œuvre de James Joyce* (Paris: Albert Messein, 1931).

_____, *We'll to the Woods No More*, trans. Stuart Gilbert (New York: New Directions, 1957).

Ellmann, Richard, *James Joyce*, rev. ed. (New York: Oxford University Press, 1982).

Epstein, Edmund L., 'James Augustine Aloysius Joyce', in Bowen and Carens, pp. 3–37.

Faerber, Thomas, and Markus Luchsinger, *Joyce in Zürich* (Zurich: Unionsverlag, 1988).

Fitch, Noel Riley, *Sylvia Beach and the Lost Generation: A History of Literary Paris in the Twenties and Thirties* (New York: Norton, 1983).

Ford, Ford Madox, *It Was the Nightingale* (Philadelphia: J. P. Lippincott, 1933).

Furbank, P. N., *Italo Svevo: The Man and the Writer* (Berkeley: University of California Press, 1966).

Gilbert, Stuart, 'Selections from the Paris Diary of Stuart Gilbert', in *Joyce Studies Annual 1990*, ed. Thomas F. Staley (Austin: University of Texas Press, 1990), pp. 3–25.

_____, *James Joyce's Ulysses: A Study* (New York: Vintage, 1955).

Givens, Seon, ed., *James Joyce: Two Decades of Criticism*, rev. ed. (New York: Vanguard, 1948).

Gogarty, Oliver St John, *As I Was Going Down Sackville Street* (London: Reynal and Hitchcock, 1937).

_____ , *It Isn't This Time of Year at All: An Unpremeditated Autobiography* (Garden City: Doubleday, 1954).

_____ , *Many Lines to Thee: Letters to G. K. A. Bell*, ed. James F. Carens (Dublin: Dolmen, 1971).

_____ , *Mourning Becomes Mrs. Spendlove and Other Portraits, Grave and Gay* (New York: Creative Age, 1948).

Gorman, Herbert, *James Joyce*, rev. ed. (New York: Rinehart, 1948).

Hayman, David, 'Shadow of His Mind: The Papers of Lucia Joyce', in Beja et al., *James Joyce: The Centennial Symposium*, pp. 193–206.

Hutchins, Patricia, *James Joyce's World* (London: Methuen, 1957).

Hyman, Louis, *The Jews of Ireland: From the Earliest Times to the Year 1910* (Shannon: Irish University Press, 1972).

James, William, *The Principles of Psychology*, two vols (New York: Dover, 1950).

Jolas, Eugene, 'My Friend James Joyce', in Givens, pp. 3–18.

Jolas, Maria, 'The Joyce I Knew and the Women around Him', *Crane Bag* 4 (1980) 82–7.

Joyce, James, *The Critical Writings of James Joyce*, ed. Ellsworth Mason and Richard Ellmann (New York: Viking, 1959).

_____ , *Dubliners*, ed. Robert Scholes in consultation with Richard Ellmann (New York: Viking, 1967).

_____ , *Exiles* (New York: Viking, 1951).

_____ , *Finnegans Wake* (London: Faber and Faber, 1971).

_____ , *James Joyce Archive: Notes, Criticism, Translations and Miscellaneous Writings*, vol. 2, ed. Hans Walter Gabler (New York: Garland, 1979).

_____ , *Letters of James Joyce*, vol. I, ed. Stuart Gilbert (New York: Viking, 1957) reissued with corrections 1966; vols II and III, ed. Richard Ellmann (New York: Viking, 1966).

_____ , *The Portable James Joyce*, ed. Harry Levin (New York: Viking, 1947).

_____ , *A Portrait of the Artist as a Young Man*, ed. Chester G. Anderson and Richard Ellmann (London: Penguin, 1980).

_____ , *Selected Letters of James Joyce*, ed. Richard Ellmann (New York: Viking, 1975).

_____ , *Stephen Hero*, ed. John J. Slocum and Herbert Cahoon (New York: New Directions, 1963).

_____ , *Ulysses*, ed. Hans Walter Gabler et al. (New York: Random House, 1986; London: Bodley Head and Penguin, 1986).

_____ , *The Workshop of Daedalus: James Joyce and the Raw Materials for A Portrait of the Artist as a Young Man*, ed. Robert Scholes and Richard M. Kain (Evanston: Northwestern University Press, 1965).

Joyce, Stanislaus, *The Complete Dublin Diary of Stanislaus Joyce*, ed. George H. Healy (Ithaca: Cornell University Press, 1971).

_____ , *My Brother's Keeper: James Joyce's Early Years*, ed. Richard Ellmann (New York: Viking, 1958).

Kain, Richard M., 'An Interview with Carola Giedion-Welcker and Maria Jolas', *James Joyce Quarterly* 11 (Winter 1974) 94–122.

Kearney, Colbert, 'The Joycead', in Beja and Benstock, *Coping with Joyce*, pp. 55–72.

Lewis, Wyndham, *Time and Western Man* (New York: Harcourt Brace, 1928).

Lidderdale, Jane, and Mary Nicholson, *Dear Miss Weaver: Harriet Shaw Weaver, 1876–1961* (New York: Viking, 1970).

Lidderdale, Jane, 'Lucia Joyce at St. Andrew's', *James Joyce Broadsheet* 10 (February 1983) p. 3.

Maddox, Brenda, *Nora: A Biography of Nora Joyce* (London: Hamish Hamilton, 1988).

Manganiello, Dominic, *Joyce's Politics* (London: Routledge and Kegan Paul, 1980).

McAlmon, Robert, *Being Geniuses Together, 1920–1930* (Garden City: Doubleday, 1968).

Melchiori, Giorgio, *Joyce in Rome: The Genesis of Ulysses* (Rome: Belzoni, 1984).

Moscato, Michael, and Leslie Le Blanc, eds, *The United States of America v. One Book Entitled Ulysses by James Joyce: Documents and Commentary – A Fifty Year Retrospective* (Frederick: University Publications of America, 1984).

Nadel, Ira B., *Joyce and the Jews: Culture and Texts* (Iowa City: University of Iowa Press, 1989).

Noel, Lucie, *James Joyce and Paul Léon: The Story of a Friendship* (New York: Gotham Book Mart, 1950).

O Clérigh, Gearòid, 'Father Dolan and Others: Joyce's Clongowes Contacts', *James Joyce Quarterly* 25 (Winter 1988) 191–206.

O'Connor, Ulick, ed., *The Joyce We Knew: Memoirs by Eugene Sheehy, William G. Fallon, Padraic Colum, Arthur Power* (Cork: Mercier, 1967).

Potts, Willard, ed., *Portraits of the Artist in Exile: Recollections of James Joyce by Europeans* (Seattle: University of Washington Press, 1979).

Pound, Ezra. *Pound/Joyce: The Letters of Ezra Pound to James Joyce, with Pound's Essays on Joyce*, ed. Forrest Read (New York: New Directions, 1967).

Power, Arthur, *Conversations with James Joyce*, ed. Clive Hart (New York: Barnes and Noble, 1974).

Reid, Benjamin L., *The Man from New York: John Quinn and His Friends* (New York: Oxford University Press, 1968).

Scott, Bonnie Kime, *Joyce and Feminism* (Bloomington: Indiana University Press, 1984).

Staley, Thomas, ed., *James Joyce Today: Essays on the Major Works* (Bloomington: Indiana University Press, 1966).

Stevens, Kenneth R., '*Ulysses* on Trial', in *Joyce at Texas: Essays on the James Joyce Materials at the Humanities Research Center*, ed. Dave Oliphant and Thomas Zigal (Austin: Humanities Research Center, 1983) pp. 91–105.

Stoppard, Tom, *Travesties* (New York: Grove, 1975).

Straumann, Heinrich, 'Four Letters to Martha Fleischmann', in *LII*, pp. 426–31.

Svevo, Italo, *James Joyce: A Lecture Delivered in Milan in 1927*, trans. Stanislaus Joyce (Norfolk: New Directions, 1950).

Thrane, J. R., 'Joyce's Sermon on Hell: Its Sources and Its Background', *Modern Philology* 57 (1960) 172–98.

Woolf, Leonard, *Beginning Again: An Autobiography of the Years 1911–1918* (London: Hogarth, 1964).

Woolf, Virginia, *The Diary of Virginia Woolf: Volume One, 1915–1919*, ed. Anne Olivier Bell (New York: Harcourt Brace Jovanovich, 1977).

_____ , *The Diary of Virginia Woolf: Volume Two, 1920–1924*, ed. Anne Olivier Bell and Andrew McNellie (New York: Harcourt Brace Jovanovich, 1978).

_____ , *The Letters of Virginia Woolf, Volume II: 1912–1922*, ed. Nigel Nicolson and Joanne Trautmann (New York: Harcourt Brace Jovanovich, 1976).

Yeats, William Butler, *Collected Poems* (New York: Macmillan, 1956).

Index

Bruni, Alessandro Francini, 45–6
Bruno, Giordano, 12, 102
Brussels, 113
Budapest, 120
Budgen, Frank, ix, 5, 58, 64, 67, 69, 71, 72, 75, 77, 79, 81, 99, 102, 131*n*, 132*n*, 133*n*
James Joyce and the Making of Ulysses, 102
Byrne, J. F., 10, 13–14, 18, 21, 24–5, 42, 50, 52, 53, 63, 65, 68, 110
Byron, Lord, 7

Calder, Alexander, 117
Callanan, Mary Ellen (JJ's second cousin), 126
Callanan, Mrs (JJ's great-aunt), 35, 126
Calypso, 64
Carr, Henry, [70], 72–3
Catholic Church, 4, 5, 9, 26, 34, 47, 51, 58, 112, 125
Catholicism, Joyce and, 8–9, 16–17, 24, 46, 47, 51, 54, 112, 125
Censorship, Joyce's problems with, viii, 12, 36–9, 60–1, 73–5, 78, 83–4, 87, 93–4, 96–9, 102, 104
Cerf, Bernard, 97–9
Cézanne, Paul, 114
Chance, Charles, 69
Chapelizod, 90
Christian Brothers school, 6
Churchill, Winston, 86
Cities, importance to Joyce of, 31–2; Also, see Dublin
Cixous, Hélène, 52, 69–70, 132*n*
Clifton School, Dalkey, 18
Clongowes Wood College, 5–7, 31, 44, 132*n*
Clongownian, 44
Coleman, Samuel C., 98–9
Coleridge, Samuel Taylor, [77]
The Rime of the Ancient Mariner, 77
Colum, Mary, 13, 21, 73, 74, 92,

96, 97, 101, 111, 112, 114–115, 116, 133*n*
Colum, Padraic, 7, 8, 28, 33, 34, 38, 39, 95, 97, 112, 114, 119, 133*n*
Conboy, Martin, 99
Conmee, Rev. John, S. J., 5–6, Also, see under James Joyce, Characters
Conrad, Joseph, 60, 89
Conroy, Mark, xi
Constant, Benjamin, 105
Conway, Mrs Hearn ('Dante'), 4–5
Copenhagen, 120
Cork, 1, 2, 6
Cosgrave, Vincent, 14, 52–3, 61, 63, 68, 80, 131*n*, 132*n*
Cowley, Malcolm, 98
Creagh, Father John, 58
'Croppy Boy, The', 19
Cullen, Father James, 8
Cummins, Margaret, 68
Cunard, Lady (Maud), 76
Curran, Constantine P., 13, 32–3, 42, 52, 108–9

Dada, 71
Daily Mirror, 111
Daly, Father James, 5
Dana, 40
Dante Alighieri, 102
Darantiere, Maurice, 85–6
Darlington, Father Joseph, 42
Delimata, Bozena Berta Schaurek (JJ's niece), 41, 49, 56, 108, 116, 118, 127, 133*n*
Delimata, Jurek (JJ's grand-nephew), 127
Delimata, Solomon (JJ's grand-nephew), 128
Delimata, Tadek (JJ's niece's husband), 127
Dempsey, George, 7
Dewey, John, 98
Dietrich, Marlene, 96
Dijon, 85–6, 97
Dillon, Eilis, 22–3